S. Hrg. 115–22

THE EFFECT OF BORROWING ON FEDERAL SPENDING

HEARING

BEFORE THE

SUBCOMMITTEE ON FEDERAL SPENDING OVERSIGHT AND EMERGENCY MANAGEMENT

OF THE

COMMITTEE ON HOMELAND SECURITY AND GOVERNMENTAL AFFAIRS UNITED STATES SENATE

ONE HUNDRED FIFTEENTH CONGRESS

FIRST SESSION

MARCH 29, 2017

Available via http://www.fdsys.gov

Printed for the use of the Committee on Homeland Security
and Governmental Affairs

U.S. GOVERNMENT PUBLISHING OFFICE

25–082 PDF   WASHINGTON : 2017

For sale by the Superintendent of Documents, U.S. Government Publishing Office
Internet: bookstore.gpo.gov   Phone: toll free (866) 512–1800; DC area (202) 512–1800
Fax: (202) 512–2104   Mail: Stop IDCC, Washington, DC 20402–0001

CONTENTS

THE EFFECT OF BORROWING ON FEDERAL SPENDING

WEDNESDAY, MARCH 29, 2017

U.S. SENATE,
SUBCOMMITTEE ON FEDERAL SPENDING,
OVERSIGHT AND EMERGENCY MANAGEMENT,
OF THE COMMITTEE ON HOMELAND SECURITY
AND GOVERNMENTAL AFFAIRS,
Washington, DC.

The Subcommittee met, pursuant to notice, at 2:33 p.m., in room 342, Dirksen Senate Office Building, Hon. Rand Paul, Chairman of the Subcommittee, presiding.

Present: Senators Paul, Lankford, Peters, and Hassan.

OPENING STATEMENT OF SENATOR PAUL[1]

Senator PAUL. I call this hearing of the Federal Spending Oversight Subcommittee to order.

Two weeks ago today, the Federal Government reached its credit limit. As a Nation, we owe almost $20 trillion, about $60,000 for each American alive now, including children. Yet we are told that $20 trillion is not that much, and that it may well grow, and that sometime soon we are going to have to ask again to raise the debt ceiling.

This is what we want to explore here today: what is our debt situation, how does it impact our budget, and how should we respond? Some argue that raising the debt should just be automatic; we really should not debate about it; that any debate or amendments would suggest the possibility of default, and that that would be dangerous.

I do not want to default, but I also think it is wrong for Congress to approve more borrowing without necessary reforms and without making it a point to try to find a chance to fix some of the situation we have.

I think it is a mistake also, though, to scare the markets and to talk of default and say default will occur if we do not have this vote immediately.

If you look at our monthly average cash-flow, the Federal Government is able to actually pay its interest on the debt, salaries for our troops, Social Security, and really much more, even if we did not raise the debt ceiling. In fact, on an annualized basis, we can fund 86 percent of government without net borrowing. So default

---

[1] The prepared statement of Senator Paul appears in the Appendix on page 31.

is not necessarily an unavoidable occurrence if the debt limit is not raised.

Now, some scholars would argue that we should not worry; we do not really need to ever pay back our debt. Keynes said not to worry about the long run because in the long run, we will all be dead.

Others have argued, the debt can be stabilized or simply inflated away. I do not share these views, but even for those who do, the one thing we cannot outlive or inflate away is the interest on our debt. This year alone, we will pay $295 billion in interest. This is more than we spend this year on seven Cabinet Departments, the White House, Congress, and the courts combined. More concerning is how ongoing deficits mean interest will consume more and more of the budget.

I want to draw attention to this chart[1] we have over here on the screen. It shows our share of Federal spending that goes to interest on the debt, discretionary spending and mandatory spending over the last 30 years.

What we see is shocking. Today, the American worker sees roughly seven cents of their tax dollar going to interest and 30 cents to discretionary spending. But by the time a recent graduate today is near retirement, interest and discretionary spending will be taking an equal share of the tax dollar, roughly 19 cents. So under the current course, interest will progressively squeeze out discretionary spending. So what do we get for interest? Really nothing, not one hour of work and not one sticky note.

Now, we always hear that spending today is an investment and that cutting anything would be too devastating. We hear this really from both sides, both the right and the left. This is not a Republican/Democrat problem. This is a both-parties problem.

We hear right and left. We are always told, "You know what? We will be fiscally responsible tomorrow," but tomorrow never comes. We simply cannot continue to rack up the debt at the rate we are.

So just two months ago, I proposed a budget that would balance in five years, without touching Social Security and without an actual spending cut. Simply by freezing spending over five years, we would balance the budget. Yet only 14 Senators had the courage to vote for such a budget.

So this brings me to my last point. Doing the right thing is hard and often not politically expedient. Congress rarely makes simple, unpleasant choices, which means we end up facing difficult and unavoidable catastrophic problems. We only act when circumstances force us to.

This is why the debt limit is important. It is our internal credit limit, not that of our creditors. It is an opportunity to reassess our spending and ask, "How did we get here, and how do we get out of this mess?" Answering those questions as part of past debt limit debates has spawned most, if not all, major Federal process reforms. The most notable example is the 1974 Budget Act, but Gramm-Rudman-Hollings, pay as you go, all of the sequester, all came out of the debt limit debates. So when people say, "Oh, no, no. We should just hurry up, hurry up and raise the debt limit

---

[1] The chart referenced by Senator Paul appears in the Appendix on page 70.

without any reforms," it is exactly wrong. It is historically wrong, and every time we have ever gotten any process reform to try to fix it, it has been with a debt limit debate. So I think we should not shy away from having a real debate when we raise the debt limit.

The Budget Act of 1974 was supposed to be an improvement and fix problems, but big spenders have over 40 years to figure it out, and they largely have evaded it now.

My hope is that, once again, as we debate raising the debt ceiling, though, that we can reform spending and have significant reforms that will put us on the right course.

With that, I would like recognize Ranking Member Peters for his opening statement, but before I do that, I would just want to note that this is Senator Peter's first hearing as Ranking Member of this Subcommittee. I would like to welcome him and I look forward to working with you. Senator Peters.

OPENING STATEMENT OF SENATOR PETERS[1]

Senator PETERS. Well, I thank you, Chairman Paul. Thank you for the welcome, and it is a pleasure to serve with you, and I look forward to having many productive hearings in the months and years ahead and for bringing us here today to discuss, certainly, this very critical topic of the national debt and the pressing matter of the debt ceiling.

I would also like to give a sincere thank-you to our distinguished panel of guests. Your perspectives on both the national debt and the debt ceiling is absolutely critical to us as policymakers.

And today, we will consider what I think are two significant, distinct, and most importantly, solvable problems.

Perhaps I am an optimist, but I am finding sustainable solutions for our Nation's debt as well as finding a path forward on the debt ceiling are both problems that can and should be solved in a responsible, bipartisan manner.

To me, working in a bipartisan manner on these issues is the only path forward. It is what I believe we were sent here to do: to find the solutions that put America on a path toward a sustainable fiscal future.

As 2017 progresses, we are going to hear many School House Rock explanations of the debt limit, the statutory and arbitrary constraint on the amount of money the U.S. Treasury can borrow.

Much of the conversation will be focused on questions like: When is the right time to talk about solutions for the long-term debt and deficits? We should be constantly working toward fiscal responsibility. This is not, and should not be, a seasonal debate, and I am sure the Chairman certainly shares that sentiment.

But just as we should be constantly engaged in discussions about how to solve our long-term issues, it is wholly irresponsible to turn this debate into one that threatens the full faith and credit of the United States.

The global economy relies on the fact that at the end of the day, no matter the chaos in the rest of the world, the U.S. Government will fulfill its obligations and pay its bills.

---

[1] The prepared statement of Senator Peters appears in the Appendix on page 35.

On March 16, 2017, under the Bipartisan Budget Act of 2015, the previously suspended debt ceiling was reinstated at just over $18 trillion. Immediately on March 16, Treasury Secretary Mnuchin wrote to Congress to inform us that the United States Treasury was taking extraordinary measures to avoid a breach in the debt ceiling.

According to analysis of the debt limit conducted by both the Congressional Budget Office (CBO) and the Bipartisan Policy Center, the Treasury Department's extraordinary measures may be able to extend the date to which the U.S. Government can fulfill its financial obligations into the fall of 2017, perhaps October or November.

However, Congress can and should immediately begin discussions to address our obligations. After having been through numerous debates on the debt limit since 2011, it would be the height of irresponsibility to let this debate slip into the midnight hour.

I remind my colleagues, while a breach of the debt ceiling would have unprecedented and potentially catastrophic, impact on the global economy, brinksmanship alone has the potential to hurt everyday working families.

In 2011, as Congress struggled to reach an agreement at the last minute, the U.S. debt was downgraded, consumer confidence fell sharply, and the stock market and credit markets took months to fully stabilize.

To some, though, the debate in Washington may seem abstract, but if we yet again engage in brinksmanship, we are jeopardizing the chance for a working-class family to purchase their first home or take out a loan to buy a much needed automobile. We are risk- ing thousands of Americans' retirement savings that they have built up over a lifetime of hard work. This is simply not acceptable. If there is to be renegotiation on the debt ceiling, I ask my col- leagues, let it happen now. We cannot afford to let our differences risk the financial future of everyday Americans. Failure to act is also not an option when it comes to long-term debt and deficit re- duction.

Solving this challenge will take bipartisan cooperation, and it will require a comprehensive approach that addresses all three fundamental factors of deficit reduction: cutting spending, reforming taxes, and investing in economic growth.

Budget plans that shift the burden onto one group at the expense of another or that ignore any of these three basic factors will not solve the problem. We need to support economic growth. We need to find real solutions to curbing long-term health care costs. We need to reform our Tax Code into one that promotes job creation and investment here at home in America. We need to make government more efficient, and we need to find responsible ways to cut spending.

I hope today serves as an open forum on these issues, both our long-term debt as well as the debt limit, and I know that each of our witnesses are very well informed and highly respected on these topics.

So I hope you use this forum to give us a very honest assessment of these challenges. We may not agree on some of the proposals that we hear, but it is only by engaging in bipartisan, collaborative fashion that we are going to find the solutions that America deserves and the American people are expecting us to come up with. Thank you.

Senator PAUL. Thank you, Senator Peters.

With that, I will begin by introducing our first witness, the Honorable David M. Walker. Mr. Walker is the former Comptroller General of the United States and head of the U.S. Government Accountability Office (GAO). He also served as president and Chief Executive Officer (CEO) of the Peter G. Peterson Foundation and founded the Comeback America initiative. Mr. Walker has written three books and is also the subject of the documentary "I.O.U.S.A.," about government debt, the topic of today's hearing.

So we are happy to have you here, and we would love to hear your thoughts on the issue. Mr. Walker.

TESTIMONY OF THE HONORABLE DAVID M. WALKER,[1] FORMER COMPTROLLER GENERAL OF THE UNITED STATES, UNITED STATES GOVERNMENT ACCOUNTABILITY OFFICE

Mr. WALKER. Thank you. Chairman Paul, Ranking Member Peters, Senator Hassan, thank you very much for the opportunity to testify today.

The title for this hearing is "The Effect of Borrowing on Federal Spending." The shorter answer is there are several implications of our current Federal spending and borrowing practices. They include, first, additional debt results and higher interest costs that can serve to crowd out other Federal spending, especially discretionary spending, and/or increase pressure for tax increases.

The CBO has projected that interest cost will be the fastest growing expense in the Federal budget on a percentage basis over the next 10 years, and what do we get for interest? As the Chairman said, nothing.

Excessive levels of debt as a percentage of the economy can serve to reduce economic growth and job opportunities. It can also cause a crisis of confidence in the U.S. dollar and much higher interest rates if the market ever decides that the Federal Government has lost control of its finances and is not willing to regain control of them.

Additional debt serves to mortgage the future of our children, grandchildren, and future generations at a time when they will face increasing competition in a much more interconnected and competitive global marketplace.

From a broader perspective, the United States has strayed from many of the key principles and values that it was founded on and which made us great. Since 1913, the Federal Government has grown from two percent of the Nation's economy to about 21 percent and increasing.

In addition, in 1913, the Congress controlled 97 percent of all Federal spending annually. The only thing they did not control was interest. Today, in fiscal 2016, 69 percent of Federal spending, including interest, was deemed to be mandatory spending. Shockingly, the 31 percent of Federal spending that was controlled included all of the express and enumerated responsibilities outlined

---

[1] The prepared statement of Mr. Walker appears in the Appendix on page 40.

for the Federal Government under the Constitution and all investments in our future.

Discretionary spending is coming under increasing pressure since mandatory spending is increasing at rates faster than the economy due to known demographic trends and rising health care costs. The bottom line is that Congress has lost control of the budget. Our debt burdens have now escalated to imprudent levels, and our collective future is now at risk.

The Federal Government is still adding debt faster than the growth rate of the economy, and interest rates have started to rise.

The CBO now estimates that interest expense will be the fastest growing category of spending, as I mentioned before, all the more reason why the Treasury Department should consider issuing 50-plus-year bonds as the GAO and I recommended over 10 years ago. Since the beginning of our Republic, there have only been two times in our history that Federal public debt as a percentage of the economy has exceeded 40 percent—at the end of World War II and the immediate aftermath and today. According to the GAO, the percentage of debt held by the public is on a path to rise to levels far in excess of the Nation's high, absent a major correction in course.

Defusing our Nation's debt bomb will require an unprecedented public education and engagement effort as a prelude to major budget, tax, Social Security, Medicare/Medicare, health care, defense, government organization operations, and yes, even political reforms.

The primary mechanism that Congress has used to control the level of debt in the past is the debt ceiling limit. However, it has not proved to be effective in limiting the growth of Federal debt, forcing a reconsideration of the proper role of the Federal Government, including the need to reform mandatory spending programs and tax expenditures.

In addition, the Federal debt, subject to the debt ceiling, will soon pass $20 trillion, which his 105 percent of gross domestic product (GDP) and 3.5 times higher than it was in the year 2000.

In my view, given the recent history, the debt ceiling limit needs to be replaced ultimately with a stronger statutory set of budget controls and a constitutional amendment that would limit public debt to GDP with specific targets and automatic enforcement mechanisms if the targets are not met.

As you Senators may be aware, there is currently an effort to achieve a State-led convention under Article V for a fiscal responsibility provision. My view is debt to GDP is vastly preferable to a balanced budget for a variety of reasons. Twenty-nine States have now ratified that out of the 34 that are required.

Speaking of the States, ultimately when the Federal Government restructures, bad news flows downhill. A typical State relies upon the Federal Government for about a third of its finances, as Senator Hassan knows having been a Governor, and we have also started to look at the financial condition and relative competitive posture of the States.

I provide in Exhibit C, the Members of this Subcommittee, their States' rank from a high of number two in relative financial position to a low of number 49. It is important that the States get their act together too.

In summary, we live in a great nation, but we have strayed from the principles and values that made us great. We are currently on an imprudent and unsustainable fiscal path. We need to be honest with ourselves and with the American people. Tough choices are required on the spending and revenue side of the budget in order to restore fiscal responsibility, enhance growth, and create a better future. The sooner we start making those choices the better, so the miracle of compounding can start working for us rather than against us as it is now.

I would be happy to answer questions after my colleagues have an opportunity to testify. Thank you again.

Senator PAUL. Thank you.

Our next witness is Veronique de Rugy, who is a Senior Research Fellow at Mercatus Center at George Mason University and a nationally syndicated columnist. In 2015, she was named the Politico Magazine's Guide to the Top 50 thinkers, doers, and visionaries transforming American politics. That is just one of her many accomplishments.

Dr. de Rugy has written extensively on the issues before this Committee today, including the dangers of our debt and the drivers of it. She has also put forward some ideas on how to get our budget in order, one of which is dear to me, the rooting out and eliminating waste.

Dr. de Rugy, thank you for being here, and we look forward to your testimony.

TESTIMONY OF VERONIQUE DE RUGY, PH.D.,[1] SENIOR RESEARCH FELLOW, THE MERCATUS CENTER, GEORGE MASON UNIVERSITY

Ms. DE RUGY. Thank you, Senator. Chairman Paul, Ranking Member Peters, and Members of the Subcommittee, thank you for the opportunity to testify before you today.

I would like to make three points. First, since the debt ceiling showdowns of 2011 and 2013, we have actually come a long way in understanding what options are available to us when a debt ceiling crisis occurs.

Second, we still need to recognize that the fights over the debt ceiling are only a symptom of a more problematic disease—government overspending. The Federal Government spends too much money, which drives the need to increase its borrowing authority so much and so regularly.

Third, the State of affairs is unsustainable. We must address the explosion and mandatory spending and, in particular, in entitlement spending. Thankfully, there are a number of institutional reforms and entitlement reforms that can be implemented to check the spending that drives the growth in our debt, and a debt ceiling debate is a good time to demand these changes.

So let me start. First, during the 2011 debt ceiling debate, my colleague Jason Fichtner and I wrote a paper that explained that when the government reaches the debt ceiling and the Treasury

---

[1] The prepared statement of Ms. de Rugy appears in the Appendix on page 49.

can no longer issue Federal debt, it would still have a way to stage off a regrettable default while giving time to Congress to reach an agreement about implementing some reforms that would get us on a more sustainable fiscal path. At the time, we explained that the Treasury Department had several financial management options to continue paying the government's obligation, including prioritizing the debt, liquidating some assets to pay government bills, and using the Social Security trust fund to continue paying Social Security benefits.

The previous administration, however, initially rejected these options, but now there are actually recognized acceptable procedures by Treasury, the Congressional Budget Office, and even the Federal Reserve of New York.

Now, I would like to note that we never advocated for any particular measures, and we often lamented that this path had to be pursued because they have a cost. However, we also noted that it was much more responsible than defaulting on our debt or raising the debt ceiling without making any changes to the State of our finances.

While there are several instances where Congress has used the debt ceiling as an opportunity, as you have said, Senator, to implement other reforms, for the most part, the debt ceiling was raised without any attempt to control spending, and the result has been a Federal debt that has ballooned from less than $5 trillion in 1993 to almost $20 trillion today and growing.

Deficits are also going up. Over the coming decades, the deficit will double to almost five percent of GDP, and CBO predicts that cumulative deficits in the next 10 years will be a total of $10 trillion.

Academic and international organizations have warned us against the negative consequences of not getting our long-term debt under control. Indeed, the consequences would be low economic growth, higher taxes, lower standard of living which would hurt the neediest of Americans, and the real threat of a debt crisis.

Real institutional reforms as opposed to a one-time cut would change the trajectory of fiscal policy and put the United States on a more sustainable path. I believe we should adopt a constitutional amendment to limit spending, but there are reforms that could be implemented immediately such as adopting a strict cut-as-you-go system or creating a Base Realignment and Closure (BRAC)-like commission for discretionary spending. However, Congress must implement reforms to take control of mandatory spending. Without reform, the rate of spending under Medicare, Medicaid, and Social Security will have devastating effects on these programs, but also other government programs in our national economy.

Again, without reforms today, vast tax increases will be needed to pay for the $75 trillion unfunded promises we have made to a steadily growing cohort of seniors.

Fortunately, many workable solutions are available to lawmakers, like turning Medicaid into a true safety net or modernizing Medicare to address fiscal and structure challenges.

Also, rather than focus just on insurance as the only solution to our country's health care challenges, we can pursue changes in regulatory policy that can generate the type of health care innovation and provider competition that can break the health care cost curve to bits rather than simply bend it temporarily.

Thank you for the opportunity to testify before you today, and I am looking forward to your questions.

Senator PAUL. Thank you.

Finally, I would like to introduce Mark Zandi. Dr. Zandi is the Chief Economist of Moody's Analytics, a well-known provider of economic research. He should be familiar to just about anyone who has followed fiscal and economic issues for any amount of time. He has testified numerous times before Congress on fiscal matters and is a regular on the financial networks.

Thank you, Dr. Zandi, for coming.

TESTIMONY OF MARK M. ZANDI, PH.D.,[1] CHIEF ECONOMIST MOODY'S ANALYTICS

Mr. ZANDI. Thank you, Chairman Paul, Senator Peters, Senator Hassan. It is very kind of you to give me the opportunity to participate today.

I should mention for sake of disclosure, I am not employed by the rating agency, Moody's Corporation is made of two entities Moody's Analytics and Moody's Investor Service. I am not part of Moody's Investor Service, the rating agency.

I am also on the board of directors of the Mortgage Guaranty Insurance Company (MGIC), a large mortgage insurer, and vice chair of the board of a nonprofit community development financial institution that makes investments across the country in underserved communities.

I would like to make three points as well. I think we have all learned that that is about as many as we can make and people can digest.

Point No. 1, you have a lot of work to do, a lot of budget issues dead ahead, one coming up in a few weeks. You will have to extent authority, spending authority for the government by the end of April.

But I think the biggest budget issue this year is the Treasury debt limit. It is very important that that is resolved in a timely way. By my calculation, this has to be done by October 5, give or take, but I do not think any longer than October 5.

Not addressing the debt limit in a timely way will be very costly. Not for a while, because I think markets have become conditioned to believe that when push comes to shove, you are going to act and solve this problem. So it is not going to be an issue today, it is not going to be an issue a month from now, but as we get closer, at some point, this is going to become a very significant issue. And it will be very costly, even if we do not breach the debt limit.

We did a study looking at the last time we went through this, back in late 2013. Interest rates did rise, as we came up to the limit. If you do a bit of work and calculation, we found that it cost taxpayers about a half a billion dollars, just that brinkmanship around the limit and the effect that it had on interest rates.

Of course, the limit was increased. If we solve that problem, the issue is resolved, and we move forward, and everything was OK.

---

[1] The prepared statement of Mr. Zandi appears in the Appendix on page 58.

But if we actually do not solve this issue and we have reached the debt limit, I do not agree. I do not think there is any way to prioritize here. Maybe you can do it in a technical sense, but effectively, I think financial markets will crater, and it will have very serious implications for economic growth, jobs, and the cost to taxpayers will be enormous, a very bad idea.

Point No. 2, I would recommend that you do away with the statutory debt ceiling. It is a bad idea. It is anachronistic and can be very disruptive. I do not think it helps in terms of making good policy decisions.

If that is a step too far, I would recommend perhaps adopting ability-to-pay rules. The idea would be that every time you have a bill for spending, taxes, annual appropriation bill, you have to make sure that you have sufficient tax, future tax revenue, and borrowing authority to be able to meet the deficit requirements as calculated by the Congressional Budget Office.

I think this would impose some discipline. You would have a debate around this issue every time you voted for a spending bill or a tax bill that added to the future budget deficit, so still very important, but it does not lead to the situation where we have coming up now and we have this drop-dead date and a lot of havoc can be created by breaching it. So I would recommend eliminating the debt ceiling, but if barring that, ability to pay.

Finally, a third point, we have very serious long-term fiscal issues. I think both of the other folks here testified and did a very nice job of explaining that, so we have to make some changes.

And I do think that will require some entitlement reform, particularly around the growth in health care cost. That is the key to Medicare/Medicaid and really the budget going forward.

But I do think the best thing we can do in the most immediate future is focus on things that can improve economic growth. Just to give you some numbers, for every .1 percentage point increase in GDP growth, that will reduce budget deficits over a 10-year period by $300 billion. So if we can enact policies, for example, that raises expected growth over the next 10 years from 2 percent per annum GDP to, let's say, 2.5 percent, that will save $1.5 trillion off the 10-year budget, $150 billion a year.

So the work you are doing now with regard to corporate tax reform, immigration reform will be very important, infrastructure. Those are the kinds of things, I think, we need to really focus on, get that done, get growth up, and that will help to address our long-term fiscal issues. They will not solve them, but that, I think, is the best approach at the current time, to focus on those things.

Thank you very much for the opportunity.

Senator PAUL. Thank you. Thank you all for your testimony.

I do not think anybody, Republican or Democrat, wants to approach default or approach the deadline, and I agree with Senator Peters. If we began working on this with advanced notice, which, we should—we are big boys and girls—we ought to be able to get it done in time.

But if you get rid of deadlines, do you get rid of sort of the impetus to do anything? And there have been reforms that have come from having the debt ceiling debate, and, actually, the reforms, I think, most of the time have been good reforms. The problem has been the people. The people do not obey their own rules, meaning Congress does not obey their own rules.

We have had five or six significant budgetary reforms—Budget Act of 1974, Gramm-Rudman-Hollings, pay as you go. I remember when I first ran, pay as you go, I think they said they broke it 700 times in the first three years. It is sort of lack of resolve on our part, both parties, and both parties have their sacred cows they want to spend money on, so the blame, there is plenty of blame to go around.

But I think if you had no limits, if you had no debt ceiling, we would have no impetus to sort of force the issue to say we have to do something about it?

Everybody knows we have this exploding entitlement problem, and nobody is doing anything about it. The only thing that ever forces us to do anything about it is the debt ceiling deadline.

In 2011, we had a big fight. The conservatives, we proposed cut cap and balance. We actually had a balanced budget that had a percentage of spending of GDP. We did not win the day, but actually, I think we forced the issue enough that we got the sequester, which I did not think was enough at the time, but turned out to probably be the best thing we did in the last 10 years. And now it has been defeated by right and left, with both sides at fault. Military wants more money, the left wants more domestic spending, and lo and behold, the sequester has been evaded every time.

I think Mr. Walker had the most important point that I heard. It is that at one time, Congress controlled 90 percent of the spending, and now nearly 70 percent of it is not under our control. The point is we have to do something about entitlements. My side is as guilty of this as the others, and some of these are simply mechanistic things.

It is demographics. It is nobody's fault. We have more older folks now and fewer younger folks. We have to figure out how to do it. We are having fewer children. We have to do something about raising the age of eligibility, and Republicans and Democrats did it together in the 1980s.

But I guess what I would like to hear from each of you is your comments on how we fix the situation, how we address the entitlement problem, or your comments on whether a process type of reform, like a Budget Control Act of 1974 or something like that, will work.

We will start with Mr. Walker, and we will work our way down.

Mr. WALKER. Well, first, I think that we have to be honest how we keep score. We have this number up here, $19.854 trillion. The real number is about $80 trillion, because when you end up looking at unfunded Social Security, Medicare, unfunded civilian/military pensions, retiree health care, environmental cleanup costs, et cetera, most of which are in the financial statements, but they are not on the balance sheet—and those numbers are bigger, and frankly, they are growing faster than this number. So we have to be honest about what the nature and scope and magnitude of the problem is.

Second, I think we also have to work with our terminology. I think sometimes we cause our own problems because we call things, for example, "entitlements." There is only two things guaranteed under the Constitution of the United States, only two: first, debt issued by the United States, which I would argue is both debt issued to the public and debt issued to the so-called trust funds; and second, Union Civil War pensions. And I think we have paid all of those. I am from Alabama. They did not guarantee our pensions. I think I know why, but those are the only things that are guaranteed.

Now, what do we do? In 2012, I went on a 10,000-mile, 27-State national fiscal responsibility bus tour, and in two States in particular—Ohio, which was a swing State in the North, and Virginia, a swing State in the South—Alice Rivlin and I addressed a demographically representative group of voters in those two States with the facts, the truth, and the tough choices, and after doing that asked them to give us electronic confidential feedback on reforms in the following areas—budget process and controls, Social Security, Medicare/Medicaid, health care, defense, taxes, government organization operations, and political reforms, specific illustrative reforms designed to get debt to GDP down to 60 percent by then, at that time, 2030, now 2035, and to be able to do it with everything on the table.

Senator PAUL. And so you asked these groups like a focus group? What did they say?

Mr. WALKER. They were demographically representative.

Senator PAUL. What did they say about raising the age of eligibility for Social Security?

Mr. WALKER. Correct. And we got 77 percent to 90-plus percent support for packages of reforms in all the areas that I just talked to you about. OK?

Senator PAUL. Including even allowing the age of eligibility to rise?

Mr. WALKER. Correct. And we were able to do it because we got them to agree first on three things. Are we on an improved and unsustainable path? Ninety-seven percent said yes after they had the full story.

Second, should our goal be to stabilize debt to GDP at a reasonable and sustainable level? That way, it is pro-growth but with fiscal responsibility. I think about 90 percent agreed on that.

And then six principles and values to guide reform: pro-growth, socially equitable, culturally acceptable, mathematical integrity, politically feasible, and meaningful bipartisan support. Now, there is details I can go into, if you want.

But after doing that, after agreeing there is a problem, here is the goal, here is the principles and values, then we showed them a range of solutions designed to achieve that. And we got 77 to 90-plus percent support. That is not how things were done in this town. OK?

Senator PAUL. It does not seem to be working here. Dr. de Rugy.

Ms. DE RUGY. I agree. It is a difficult act to follow, and I agree entirely with what you were saying. It is interesting because it echoed a lot of polling that I have seen also that shows that when you actually present people with the tradeoffs, when you say, for instance, "Do you want this government service?" people will say, "Oh, yes." "Do you want more of it?" "Oh, yes." But when you say, "At which price?" then people are more willing to start actually talking about the kind of tradeoffs they would be willing, what they would be willing to sacrifice, whether they actually would want to see that program cut.

So it is kind of interesting, and I think, unfortunately, in this town, there is not a lot of interest to talk about real tradeoffs.

The other thing that is pretty clear is we know how to reduce debt-to-GDP ratio. First, we know there is an impact on growth, and I agree that we need to grow the economy, but we are not going to get our way. I agree that it is a priority, and it is a priority for everyone, but we cannot overstate how important it is for low-income Americans to see the economy grow.

But if you want to reduce debt to GDP—we are not going to grow ourself out of this debt. We are going to have to address our spending, and we know how to reduce our debt-to-GDP ratio. If you do a review of the literature on fiscal adjustments, what you find is that the countries that have actually implemented fiscal adjustment packages, that are made mostly of spending cuts and particularly and not surprisingly of the social transfers, the so-called entitlement spending, which you are totally right—I mean, we know we are not entitled to them; that has been proven by the Supreme Court, and Congress can just change the law at any time—those countries actually manage to reduce their debt-to-GDP ratio.

On the other hand, countries that try to do kind of a halfway thing of raising taxes and cutting spending did not succeed, and one of the reasons is because they would raise taxes and not really follow through on the spending. And they would not actually do the spending cuts where they needed to be, meaning do fundamental structural changes.

And the thing that is important is that—so we know what to do. There is multiple ways to do it, multiple solutions, and what is important is also going back to economic growth. There is always a lot of people saying, "Well, if you implement these type of packages"—right?—"it is going to have a depressive effect on the economy." Well, actually, economists agree. There is a consensus that in the long term, it is actually beneficial for the economy. And there is still a debate on the consequences in the short term.

But the question is like—while I will agree also with Mr. Zandi that, yes, reaching the debt ceiling or even have some of these conversations or getting that close has a cost. In a sense, we are getting a taste of what is going to happen to the American people if we do nothing, and it is just like simply pushing back and kicking the can down the road—and the name that it has a cost today— is irresponsible, and we absolutely need to do something.

And if I can say one more thing, reducing the cost of health care is important, and unfortunately, a lot of the conversation in this time is actually—places focus in the wrong place. Constantly talking about how we can reform the way we provide health insurance is the wrong thing to talk about. I am not saying it is not important, but it kind of ignores the fact that third-party payer, whether it is the government or insurance, actually contributes to the problem.

One of the things that would be better to do is, sure, the government provides for the neediest in terms of health coverage, but also bring as much innovation and free the supply side of health care in order to bring the kind of emulation that we have seen in other sectors like technology and many other sectors, which raises quality and reduces prices. And that is, unfortunately, a conversation we are not having enough.

Senator PAUL. Dr. Zandi.

Mr. ZANDI. I will give you four suggestions. This first suggestion is I do not think I would use the debt limit as a way to effectuate change. It is a matter of benefit and cost, and I think the costs are very significant, particularly if you breach the debt limit. We have obviously not gotten there yet, but the costs there are obviously uncertain, unknown. But a prudent planner would want to go down that path, and therefore, it is not really credible to think that is going to have a significant effect on the behavior in terms of solving these long-term fiscal issues. It is a judgment, but I think the costs there could be quite substantive and should not be discounted, particularly given the uncertainty around those costs.

The second thing I would say is, at this point in time, I think, just to reiterate the point in my oral remarks, I would focus on growth. You are thinking about policies that could help promote growth. Corporate tax reform is a very good idea. I think immigration reform is the most obvious way. More highly skilled immigrants into the country is the most obvious way to lift growth and address our long-term fiscal issues, as you brought to your point about demographics. And infrastructure spending is also key.

Third, if I were King for the Day and you are focusing on Social Security and how you would solve that and you are proposing raising the age of retirement, the path I would take would be different. I would say let's raise the payroll cap. It has eroded over time. When Social Security was put on the plan in the 1930s, it was 90 percent-plus of eligible earnings. Now we are down to 80. Let's just put it back to 90.

And the second thing I would do is I would adopt a chain-weighted Consumer Price Index (CPI). That would affect Social Security benefits. It would also affect the Tax Code and some of the parameters in the Tax Code.

So if I were going to solve Social Security, if that is what you are focused on, those are the kinds of things I would do before raising the retirement age.

Finally, the real solution in my view to solving our long-term fiscal issues is really the growth in the cost of health care. That is the key thing, but that is not going to be something you are going to solve today, next year, or the year after, just given the situation that we are in and the politics of all this.

So my advice would be let's do these other things. They are doable. They will have significant benefits. And let's come back to this when we are a few years down the road and take another crack at it because these long-term fiscal problems, they are not going away. They are here for 20, 30, 40 years. Let's do what we can do, not beat our heads against some of these other smaller things that are not going to really make a difference. It is really about the growth in health care cost.

Senator PAUL. Senator Peters.

Senator PETERS. Thank you, Mr. Chairman, and again, thank you to the panelists, your testimony, and the conversation that we are having here, it is refreshing to have a hearing like this where we can really just have a conversation back and forth, not as for- mal as these usually are. I appreciate the frankness of all of you. First off, Mr..Walker, I listened with great interest in the panels that you held around the country with a variety of groups. I lis- tened to that with interest because I have done that myself in my district, not for a few years, but a few years ago, we had a number of sessions where we had cross-sections of folks. A lot of this was a few years ago when I was in the House, the Tea Party movement was in full bloom, and the folks who were there were heavily rep- resented. Tea Party folks were heavily represented, but it was all sorts of groups of people who came together.

I will tell you my results were different than your results at each of those meetings, where there was not that sort of consensus that came out of it, as folks were saying we added the tax element, you talked about a little bit, Mr. Walker. But folks were all for tax cuts. They thought those were pretty good until they realized it was not solving their issue with the deficit, and they could not do that. Then when it talked about cuts, most of them were all in favor of cutting foreign aid. That was the top of their list, but they realized that did not have much impact whatsoever on the budget.

They were not really excited about cutting Social Security or Medicare, and so in the end of it, we did not get that kind of con- sensus. I would love to talk with you more at some point in the fu- ture as to how we bring folks together because that is kind of the crux of the problem. How do we bring America together to have this kind of comprehensive adult conversation that we need to have and understand in order to deal with this? I always explain that this is a three-legged stool. We cannot talk about dealing with the deficit unless we are dealing with all three legs, which are tax pol- icy, spending, and growth. None of those by themselves will work. You cannot raise taxes enough to deal with it. You cannot cut enough to deal with it, and you cannot grow yourself out of it. You have to do all three, and that is where you then run into the poli- tics of people just wanting tax cuts. They do not want to have any- thing that is revenue-neutral or raises more revenue or they think we can grow our way out. I think that has been pretty clear by our panelists that this is a complex issue that we have to handle, par- ticularly when you are dealing with entitlements.

I have heard a couple of you say that we know that these are not entitlements. I will tell you, ask any person of my constitu- ents—and I agree with them. These are entitlements. These are things that people have paid in their entire life, and if you tell them that they have paid into a system for their entire life, that they should get something back, like their pension plan. If they have been contributing to their pension plan and to say, "Well, we have changed the rules. We know you have paid into this for the last 30 years, and we know you are counting on a dignified retire- ment, but, hey, we changed the rules," that is not something that is going to be palatable to nearly everybody. And I agree if you pay into the system, those are the rules, and you played by the rules, you should expect that it will actually be there for you.

So these are things that we grapple with and why it is difficult to bring all of our colleagues together, but let me ask a more specific question on the debt limit to Dr. Zandi.

You have talked about the costs associated with debt limit—because we have to figure out how to force this. I agree with all three of you. We have to force these kinds of decisions. I would agree with the Chairman. We have to force this, but the question is, is this tool the appropriate one? Because I am afraid we are heading toward another crisis, and the pattern has not been very good, that we have actually had these kinds of frank discussions.

I agree. I do not think we are likely to eliminate the debt limit. That is probably not going to happen, but I think we should understand the costs associated with it.

You talked about the impact of the markets and the cost of the last crisis—although I know in your testimony, you also talked about the fact that markets are now starting to realize Congress should just do this. This is all games that they play, and they go back and forth, and it is just another example of the dysfunction that exists in the U.S. Congress that we get to those crises, but they are going to just pass it as soon as it comes to that crisis point.

So my question is, if that is the case, is this even losing its viability as a tool, and the fact that in the past, the markets would react negatively? My colleagues would say, "Oh, my gosh, we better do something here because the markets are performing badly. This is having an impact on the economy."

Mr. ZANDI. Yes.

Senator PETERS. "We better get our act together." But now it is not like we are even getting that pressure until the very end, and then it is too late. And then it could be catastrophic, potentially. Is that a fair assessment of where we are and why this is kind of a dangerous thing to be thinking about right now?

Mr. ZANDI. Yes. That is an excellent point. I mean, if you think back to the 2011 experience, December 2011—you mentioned that in your opening remarks about the downgrading of the debt by Standard & Poor's (S&P)—as soon as the letter was written by—I believe it was Treasury Secretary Geithner—I cannot remember to whom Congresswoman Pelosi—the markets had already started to react. You could actually see it in the markets, and the tension in markets started to build pretty quickly.

And that you would think started to put pressure on policymakers, "Oh, we have to do something here, or otherwise markets are going to cave."

But now they have been conditioned. We have gone down this path a number of times, again in 2013, and the letter was sent. Secretary Mnuchin sent a letter to House Speaker Ryan, and no one is even talking about it. It is like, literally, no one is talking about it. This would have been news in 2013 and big news in 2011. So I think the markets are being conditioned here to expect that you finally solve this, and there is no pressure. The markets do not react. The stock prices are not going down. The credit spreads are not gapping out. The credit default swaps spread are not widening. Where is the pressure?

But at some point—and there will be a point—everyone is going to wake up and say, "Oh, my gosh, what is going on?" Boom. And at that point, it is going to be very costly to taxpayers because we are all going to pay—we are talking about interest on the debt. Well, interest rates are going to spike, and it is going to cost us. All that short-term money that the Treasury issues is going to be issued at a much higher interest rate, and that is going to cost tax-payers. And to what end? We are going to do something with the Treasury debt limit, and everyone knows it. So I am not sure—again, it is a matter of judgment, but my sense is this is not the way to achieve the kinds of things you want to achieve here, and it could be very costly.

Senator PETERS. Just before I get to Mr. Walker, if I may, the complacency works, I think, two ways. One is that policymakers think, "Well, we do not have the pressure because the markets are not reacting this way to do it," and then there is the complacency not to do anything. Then there is also the feeling, "Well, then maybe it is OK if we breach the debt limit because the markets do not seem to be reacting to any of this."

Mr. ZANDI. Right.

Senator PETERS. If we are not seeing any pressure and then it adds to the danger level as well—and we heard a lot of conversa-tions, "Well, the markets really are not reacting. Maybe we can find other ways to get through this and prioritize," which I think is potentially very problematic. Mr. Walker.

Mr. ZANDI. Can I make one other point? We actually did default on debt briefly because of a technical mistake, it was back in early 1970s, where the Treasury, because of a computer glitch, did not actually pay on time. And there has been academic research that shows that, in fact, that raised interest rates for a very long period of time, just that technical error.

So if you actually get to a point where we do not pay, that would be very costly to us, and at the end of the day, the triple-A credit of the United States is the bedrock of the global financial system. We just should not mess around with that. That is a given, and messing around with that could be very significantly costly.

Senator PETERS. My time expired, but we want to hear from you.

Mr. WALKER. A couple things quickly. First, I used to be a trust-ee of Social Security and Medicare, one of the prior hats that I had.

While Social Security, you are paying a payroll tax during your working life and while Part A under Medicare, you are paying a payroll tax during your working life and so is the employer, you are not for B and D. Part B and Part D under Medicare are the ones that are the most underfunded, and people do not pay for that until they are actually eligible for the program to begin with. And most of the costs of those programs are funded out of general revenues.

Second, I think the big difference between the results that you got in your session and I got is that you did not have a representa-tive group of voters. You basically had adverse selection, people who wanted to come, including the extremes tend to come dis-proportionately. And so having a representative group was impor-tant to try to get better results because, unfortunately, the ex-tremes from both sides tend to be disproportionately represented in our political process.

The last thing is the process matters, and I will give you one example. In 1998, President Clinton wanted to reform Social Security, and that was right before I was appointed as Comptroller General of the United States. And I had been a trustee of Social Security and Medicare. The American Association of Retired Persons (AARP) and the Concord Coalition came together, worked with the White House to try to do several forums, where experts like myself stated the facts, spoke the truth, talked about the options, engaged people with electronic confidential balloting, and the elected officials observed. They did not talk; they observed. That resulted in some dramatic evidence that people were willing to accept some tradeoffs, and I believe that we would have had Social Security reform before the beginning of this millennium had there not been a personal problem of the President, which caused him to lose political capital.

Quite frankly, the kind of reforms that we would have done back then, because I was part of that, pretty much can be the same kind of reforms that ultimately we do. The question is, When are we going to do it?

Senator PETERS. Thank you.

Mr. WALKER. The process matters.

Senator PETERS. Right. Thank you, Mr. Walker. Thank you.

Senator PAUL. Senator Hassan.

OPENING STATEMENT OF SENATOR HASSAN

Senator HASSAN. Well, thank you, Chairman Paul and Ranking Member Peters. I am really glad to be here for my first Federal Spending Oversight and Emergency Management Subcommittee hearing. It is a privilege to join this Subcommittee, and thank you to the panelists. It is nice to see you again, Mr. Walker.

I do have a couple of questions. First, starting with Dr. Zandi, I would like to talk about the cost of government defaults and shutdowns and how that impacts our national debt. In your testimony, you warn that if the Treasury were to default on its obligations, the economic impact would be devastating, potentially more severe than the Great Recession.

In addition to the incredible damage that would cause to our families and businesses in New Hampshire and all around the country, it seems to me that the damage to our economy—you estimated a possible five percent decline in GDP—would also reduce tax revenues and then, therefore, increase the national debt considerably. Is that an assessment you agree with?

Mr. ZANDI. Yes. That is exactly right, and that was a scenario where we breached the limit. So October 5 is the limit.

Senator HASSAN. Right.

Mr. ZANDI. We breach it, and we go on for another month without resolving it, and we do not make Social Security payments. And that is the scenario that you are describing.

And you are right. Just to give you a context, the 5 percent decline in GDP that you cited for the scenario is equal to roughly the decline during the Great Recession. In the Great Recession, the debt-to-GDP ratio of the United States rose by 35 to 40 percentage points, so that gives you a sense of the magnitude of that kind of a recession and what kind of impact it would have on the budget.

Senator HASSAN. OK. So that description is one of the reasons I am hopeful that both parties can come together to deal with the debt ceiling well before the deadline, without manufacturing a crisis by bringing in unrelated political issues that really force impossible choices. I think people in both parties would agree that they get put in a situation when political issues get added on.

I am also concerned that government shutdowns can have much of the same effect. I lived through the shutdown in 2013 as the Governor of New Hampshire, watching the White Mountains National Forest shut on Columbus Day weekend, which is one of our prime tourist periods in the State.

To that point, Dr. Zandi, you previously said that the 2013 government shutdown resulted in a $20 billion hit to our Nation's GDP, as default shutdowns have a real impact on families and businesses and also reduced tax revenues, once again, increasing our national debt.

So, Dr. Zandi, do you agree that costly shutdowns increase the Federal debt, and that if Congress is serious about cutting the deficit and reducing our debt, as I am, that we should be avoiding those kind of costly defaults and shutdowns that hurt our bottom line?

Mr. ZANDI. Yes, absolutely. Just to give you a rule of thumb, for every week that the government shuts down, it costs 20 basis points of annualized GDP growth. So you can do the arithmetic.

And here is another really good rule of thumb. For every lost dollar of GDP, the deficit will increase by 40 to 50 cents. So the arithmetic here is pretty daunting.

Senator HASSAN. Well, thank you. I am truly hopeful that the threat of these kinds of consequences will help ensure that Senators from both sides of the aisle can come together and work out a clean budget deal without any poison pills.

This is a question to the full panel, as it is a related point. Dr. Zandi notes in his testimony that political uncertainty in Washington is already very high and has been since the shutdown in 2013. As this uncertainty grows, businesses are more reluctant to invest or hire workers. Families become more cautious in their spending, and GDP growth slows.

So if each of you could address how uncertainty can impact economic growth and long-term investment, and can you discuss how Congress creates uncertainty when it passes short-term continuing resolutions (CR) rather than annual appropriations or when it threatens defaults or shutdowns for political purposes?

And, Mr. Walker, I would start with you.

Mr. WALKER. Believe it or not, I am 65 years old. Congress has passed timely budget and appropriation bills four times in 65 years. That is an F minus. OK?

Business relies upon some reasonable ability to predict what the future might be, and the absence of that reasonable ability to predict, there is a cost. There is clearly an economic cost. There is clearly an opportunity cost, et cetera, and so clearly, we need budget reforms.

Frankly, the only thing under the Constitution of the United States that is express and enumerated for both houses of the Congress to do every year there is only one and that is appropriations. Yet it does not do it.

At the same point in time, rules like pay-as-you-go rules are not adequate because that assumes that we are in a sustainable position, and all we need to do is pay for new stuff when, in fact, we cannot afford what we already have.

So I think, yes, we need more certainty, but we also need to start treating the disease——

Senator HASSAN. Yes.

Mr. WALKER [continuing]. Rather than the symptoms, and that is part of what this hearing is all about.

Senator HASSAN. Thank you. Doctor.

Ms. DE RUGY. I mean, I agree. Uncertainty is a problem. Markets do not like uncertainty. It creates paralysis, but I will also say that, It is not the only way by adopting continuing resolution, time and time again, that Congress creates uncertainty.

The Tax Code is replete with temporary tax provisions, which require to be extended or not. I mean, the drama every so often over the tax extenders—it was supposed to be a one-time thing in 1988, and it has been happening all the time ever since, creates uncertainty. Writing massive regulations that will take years to write all the regs create massive amount of uncertainty. So the government has this tendency of, yes, creating massive uncertainty, and it is not a good thing.

That being said, I will say again there is no doubt, so default shutdowns are not—they are not desirable things at all. The waiting is not an option. The government is not going to meet its promises under any circumstances right now, and it is certainly not going to meet its promises with this level of debt.

Take Social Security, for instance. When the trust funds are empty, we know what is going to happen. By law, benefits are going to be cut by 25 percent. We know this, and people, the lowest-income Americans, those who really truly depend on Social Security are going to be hurting. And the idea that we can push that can down the road because Congress is going to change the law, once again, I think is foolish because by then, the debt-to-GDP ratio will be 150 percent. It is going to be already $30 trillion gross debt in 2017, 140 percent. I do not think you guys will have the luxury of actually changing the law to say we keep everything.

So I just think that I would rather for my children and future generations that we assume—I mean, that we are responsible today and start passing the reforms, and if we need to do it by using the debt ceiling, again, there are ways to not default. The idea of threatening of default all the time as if, and which is, by the way, the conversation in 2011 was one where there was no way to actually use extraordinary measures. There was no way to do prior writing—I mean, it is not that these are desirable things, but it is not true. We know it is not true, and if it allows us to not continue pushing this can down the road—in the name of my children, I would rather take that risk and rock the boat a little bit today.

Senator PAUL. Thank you. Senator Lankford.

OPENING STATEMENT OF SENATOR LANKFORD

Senator LANKFORD. Thank you.

Can we set some context real quick? When we are talking about interest and debt issues, what do you anticipate the interest payments will be 10 years from now for the United States?

Ms. DE RUGY. Can I tell you?

Senator LANKFORD. Go ahead.

Ms. DE RUGY. Right now, projected by CBO, it is going to be close to $800 billion. That assuming that the interest rates stay what it is projected to be modest.

Senator LANKFORD. Right, modest growth. Modest growth in interest rates.

Ms. DE RUGY. So almost $800 billion.

Senator LANKFORD. Mr. Walker, anything you want to mention?

Mr. WALKER. That sounds right. Right. That is modest growth in interest rates, not returning to the levels of the 1990s, by the way, but below that. Interest rate risk is arguably one of our highest risks. It is the fastest-growing expense on a percentage basis, and we get nothing for it.

Senator LANKFORD. Right. It has been one of the areas that I try to push a lot of people that I talk to, to say it is the creeping element in the budget that no one can pay attention to because you assume it is never going to get that high, but it is coming. It actually squeezes out all discretionary spending just for interest, which we will do.

So let me ask a question: How are other nations handling issues like debt limits?

Mr. WALKER. I do not know of any other nation that has a debt limit. There are nations that have what I advocated, which is a debt-to-GDP limit, with automatic targets and triggers and enforce- ment mechanisms if you violate it. Things have to happen. Right now, things do not happen, and so, as a result, we have gone from $5.7 trillion in total debt, subject to the debt ceiling limit, to almost $20 trillion since 2000. And we still have not done anything to deal with the structural driver of the fiscal imbalance.

Mr. ZANDI. Yes. Relative to other developed economies, we have a very anachronistic, unusual approach to this. There is no other country that has anything that comes close to a debt limit or even shuts the government down over these issues.

Senator LANKFORD. Right. So I asked the same question to several other international leaders last year and I was aware there is no debt limit out there anywhere else in the world, that we do it very different. But I asked a question of another international leader and said, "What happens if you get to the end, and then you tip over, and you have a government shutdown?" He laughed. He said, "We have a new election the next week, because all of us are out. Parliament dissolves, and everybody is out and done. This did not work, and we are all gone. That is how we handle it, to be able to make sure that we actually take advantage of our responsibility."

Mr. ZANDI. And, of course, they do not. So if you look at the debt to GDP of almost every developed economy in the world, it is higher than the United States at this point in time.

Senator LANKFORD. Right.

Ms. DE RUGY. I was going to say, I mean, it is hard to think of a country we should use as a model, so I think a debt ceiling or not is really——

Senator LANKFORD. So the question is the combination of several things here. I have proposed several areas to be able to get on top of this. Several Members of this Committee have as well. One is we have to avoid the constant fear of a government shutdown. That does not help us. That does hurt our economy every single time. We have to have a way to be able to solve that, but we also have to be able to bring fiscal responsibility.

I have a bill called the Government Shutdown Prevention Act, which puts the consequences on Congress and the executive branch, holds harmless every other agency, but puts the pressure where the pressure should be for us to get to appropriations, and so we can finally get to doing appropriations bills and to be able to move on.

I have noticed in the short time that I have been here that Congress only acts when it has a deadline. If there is no deadline, we never seem to get to action items; hence, things like immigration reform and so many things we discuss year after year. But with no deadline, there is no time to do it. That is why a debt ceiling suddenly creates this false deadline. That is why you have all these other entities when you deal with budget times, that it creates a deadline. So it is important, I think, that we actually accomplish something with that to be able to move, to not have a shutdown, to be able to keep maintaining where we are, but to be able to solve some of the issues.

I want to ask about the issue about a debt ceiling. I believe Congress will always expand the debt ceiling. We will find a way every time to do it for fear of default and what that means internationally to the international economies. The question is, Is it useful to us to be able to actually accomplish something with it and to be able to find a way to be able to say, how do we get hold of our interests and our debt payments at some point?

So, Mr. Walker, you have mentioned several times debt to GDP or other mechanisms. Is there a way that we can deal with a debt-ceiling vote that also has a marker on it saying the debt ceiling increases if our deficit numbers decrease by a certain percentage? So let's say Congress were to say, at this point, two years from now, our deficit decreases 10 percent. Then the debt ceiling increases, and it sets specific targets for Congress to be able to work toward. When trying to work toward this, not just we have debt-ceiling votes, because I think we are always going to have debt-ceiling votes, and there will be a way that Congress finds to pass it every time, but to have a meaningful process that is a marker to say, "We are failing to get on top of this. How do we get us back to balance and to start bringing this down?"

Mr. WALKER. If you are going to have metrics—and I am for metrics and mechanism—targets, triggers, and enforcement mechanisms—I really think you ought to change, rather than deficits and rather than total debt, to go to debt to GDP. And why do I say that? That is what really matters. That way, you could pursue pro-growth policies, and we have talked about a number, but you have to have fiscal constraint. And that fiscal constraint requires everything to be on the table. It requires discretionary spending to be on the table. It requires mandatory spending to be on the table, and it requires tax expenditures to be on the table, which is $1.2 trillion a year and largely not looked at, at all. So I think you need to move toward that approach.

The other thing, there is a group that I am the national co-founder of. It is called No Labels, and one of the things that it advocated with regard to the budget and appropriations process is no budget, no pay. That if the Congress does not pass a budget and the appropriations bills by a certain date, that Congress does not get paid until it does.

Now, there are States that have done that. I think California is one of them, and they have not had a problem since then. They have other problems.

Senator LANKFORD. Lots.

Mr. WALKER. But they do not have that problem.

Senator LANKFORD. I would not exactly pull California as a model on efficiency in spending.

Mr. WALKER. No, no, no. No, they are not, but they are ranked number 40 out of——

Senator LANKFORD. But they have found way—and not to go pick on California because their folks are not here to be able to defend themselves. But what their legislators had done as a result of that is find a way to be able to hide their debt in other places and to be able to bury it in other ways.

Mr. WALKER. And we do that too.

Senator LANKFORD. I agree. That has been the challenge that I have faced, and when you do a debt to GDP, every time you do debt to GDP, there is some way to be able to fudge the numbers and to be able to fudge exactly which GDP number that is and how you figure it and what you do. I am trying to find a way that you cannot fudge the numbers.

So when I look at specific targets—I understand economic growth has got to be a major priority, but if you look at percentage, reduction of the deficit, that assumes you are going to find a way to have economic activity and growth. You are going to have to control spending. You are going to have to find a way to be able to do that. Whether it is revenue or whether that is cutting, you have to find a way to be able to do that, but that is a clean number. That if you set a date, you cannot fudge it.

And in this town, everyone fudges the numbers. I am trying to find a clean way to say let's do a number no one can hide.

Mr. WALKER. It may have to be a transition. Yes. You may have to do something like that.

Ms. DE RUGY. Can I add something about fudging?

Senator LANKFORD. Sure.

Ms. DE RUGY. You are so right. I mean, like debt-to-GDP limit has not worked for Europe very well.

Mr. WALKER. It is because they do not enforce it.

Ms. DE RUGY. Yes, they do not enforce it. But it ultimately boils down to this: implementation. And how do you tie the hands of Congress? That is a real—that is a $20 trillion, going on $40 trillion question, is how do you tie the hands of Congress? That is really hard.

I just wanted to say something about tax expenditure. I do not entirely disagree with you, but we have to be very careful. Now those $1.2 trillion should be on the table because some of those tax expenditures are meant to mitigate the double taxation that exists in the Tax Code. So I think we have to be careful and not looking at them all as a potential source of revenue, unless we fundamentally reform our Tax Code and adopt a flat tax and get rid of double taxation of saving and——

Senator LANKFORD. I am over time, but let me make one quick comment. Where we are right now in budgeting, I am not sure it is how do you tie the hands of Congress. It is how do you untie the hands of Congress because most everything is on autopilot around here, and if you get to the end of a budget year, you do a continuing resolution. Even discretionary spending ends up being on autopilot. So this is a matter of giving Congress a deadline when they have to act and do something and cannot just sit back and say status quo will work and status quo is driving us over the cliff.

Mr. ZANDI. I have a suggestion for it if you want to hear it.

So the ability-to-pay rules in every piece of legislation, that adds to projected budget deficit. So ability to pay is equal to projected tax revenues plus borrowing authority must cover the deficits the CBO expects over the 10-year budget horizon, and that would be for every piece of legislation. That would add to future budget deficits. So every time you vote for a piece of legislation that will add to deficits, you have to also vote for the borrowing authority to achieve that.

Senator LANKFORD. How is that different than the PAYGO rules that already exist that are waived by Congress routinely?

Mr. ZANDI. If you waive them, you waive them, but that would be a rule that instead of having a Treasury debt limit, where it is cataclysmic if you go over it and, therefore, it is not credible that you will go over it, then you have this is something that would impose discipline every single time you voted for something.

Senator PAUL. Thank you. I think that illustrates a lot of the problem, is it is not that we have not tried, not that we do not have processes in place. It is a people problem.

Senator LANKFORD. Right.

Senator PAUL. We do not obey our own rules.

But I think Mr. Walker made a good point earlier when he said that basically 70 percent of the budget is not controlled by us. We need to untie our hands. We need to have our hands in all of it, but we just let the mandatory spending go on and on and on.

I actually think there are some things we could do. I mean, Democrats and Republicans did raise the age of eligibility back in 1983, and they raised taxes. Really, to my mind, as far as Social Security, we had a bill that I put forward six years ago. Two-thirds of the problem was fixed by raising the age over like a 20-or 30-year period. That fixed two-thirds of the shortfall. The remaining third, we did by means testing. You could argue whether you should raise the taxes or means-test it. They are still taking the bite from the wealthy more. The only reason I prefer means testing over taxes is means testing is on the tail end when you are not really creating jobs. You have all your wealth, and you just take a little bit less Social Security. Taxes on the early side, I think, can have a disruptive effect on the market if we tax everybody on the full extent of their wealth.

I would rather have rich people get a lot less Social Security to pay for it, but you can fix it. I do not think those are emotional things, but we just keep putting it off.

But how come we do not fix it? Senator Peters, tell us how to fix it and why we do not fix it.

Senator PETERS. So now that I am a member of the panel. [Laughter.]

Senator PAUL. It is a friendly question.

Senator PETERS. It is a friendly question.

Well, I think when you talked about some of the things related to Social Security reform, one of the increasing the age limit, the problem with that is that not everybody can work longer. It is a situation for those of us who are blessed to be able to sit at a desk in an air-conditioned environment and engage in our profession. I think many of us will probably work beyond 70 years old for obvious reasons.

A lot of the folks I represent lift heavy objects for a living, and their body does not necessarily last until 70 years. They are outside in the cold and the extremes, and so it does have a disproportionate impact based on what people's jobs are. So I find there is generally more acceptance for raising the retirement age for folks who are in office jobs and who are usually very well paid versus everyday folks who are struggling and are concerned about that.

The problem is the underlying premise, and Dr. Zandi mentioned this fact. When Ronald Reagan and that group figured they would solve Social Security for the future, they came together bipartisan. It was a great compromise. They came together. But as you mentioned, roughly 90 percent of all income was captured by that Social Security tax that paid in. It was based on the premise that everybody pays in, everybody gets it back. It captures most of the revenue.

But what has happened since those Reagan years, as we all know, is that there has been an acceleration of income inequality at an accelerating rate. So it is the fact that the folks at the very top have now—I do not have the numbers in front of me here, but a very large percentage of total income goes to the folks at the very top. If you really want to solve—the ideal way to solve Social Security in my mind is you raise everybody's income up—we get back to the 90 percent so we do not have this great gulf of not only income inequality but of wealth inequality, which is even greater than the income inequality, which causes the problem.

So to have a means test would generate revenue, but you would need to generate an awful lot from that means test. It would not be just not getting your Social Security. That would not be enough, in my mind. I would have to run the numbers. You probably have run the numbers. It is not going to make up the difference, given the fact that you have had such a drop in the amount of income that is covered because of growing inequality. So that is why it has to be more comprehensive.

Let me ask a question of the panel, after I have answered the question from the Chair. Mr. Walker, you wanted to make a comment. Do that as well, please. But as I mentioned in my opening question, this is a three-legged stool. We have not talked a lot about taxes, and yet that is actually what is pending before us here or likely to be pending before us in Congress very shortly as we look at tax reform. There are folks who would like to see if there is tax reform, and there are certainly ways that we should make this Tax Code a lot more efficient. We should get rid of this thick document and simplify it—I am all about that. We should bring more certainty and deal with some of the uncertainties associated with that.

I do not know how we deal with this if we are not dealing with at least deficit-neutral. We probably need to do more than deficit-neutral as long as we are also cutting spending and growing the economy, but we will probably need to raise some revenue, ideally. But at a minimum, we should be deficit-neutral, and we will only make this problem worse.

If you look at President Trump's proposal, it was in the trillions of dollars, at least during the campaign, which does not seem like it fixed the problem. Folks around here love to give tax cuts. That is a fun thing to go back home, but it is increasing the deficit dramatically, and that is more abstract. But we know it is very real. It is not abstract in terms of the everyday world that we live in. So to kind of get your sense on this tax proposal, are you concerned if it is something other than at least deficit-neutral?

Dr. Zandi, you are shaking your head, but I would like all of you to respond to it. Dr. Zandi.

Mr. ZANDI. Sure. I would be supportive of revenue-neutral corporate tax reform. I think the House Republican plan, the proposal that has been put forward by Congressman Brady, is a pretty good plan. There are things to be worried about, particularly with regard to the border adjustment tax and some of the issues around transition and whether it violates WTO rules. But broadly speaking, on a reasonably dynamically scored basis, that would be a reasonable proposal. It is revenue-neutral, roughly.

Other than that, I would not be supportive of cuts in personal income taxes at that point, unless you could do revenue-neutral kind of taxation to lower marginal rates and broaden the base. But I think that should be the key criteria that this—when it is all said and done, currently Federal revenue to GDP is 19 percent. That is where it should be. I think we should work toward that and try to make the Tax Code more efficient, work for us in a better way, promote growth, but I do not think we should reduce it. That has been the average amount of revenue raised, and as a percent of GDP for 35 or 40 years, I do not think that should at this point in time.

Ms. DE RUGY. I agree with you that tax cuts should be deficit-neutral, not revenue-neutral, and there is just a lot of things we could cut, especially if we are talking about 10 years. The House Republican bill is a good bill, especially the growth, the part that grows the economy, but the border adjustment tax is actually a terrible idea. It is something that is completely untested, with extremely large amount of risks. And I could go on and on and on about this.

But I think the goal—and outside the border adjustment, there is other ways in the bill, other provisions to raise revenue. I think a proper tax reform will do a little bit. If you cut some rates, you expand the base, so you do some revenue increase too. But I think deficit neutrality should be the goal, not revenue neutrality.

Senator PETERS. If I may just briefly.

Ms. DE RUGY. Yes.

Senator PETERS. Your opposition to the border tax, if that is taken out, the math does not work real well for the tax plan. Do you agree or——

Ms. DE RUGY. Yes. It does not work. It does not work really. That is true.

Senator PETERS. At all, in fact.

Ms. DE RUGY. But you could do a smaller package too. This discussion right now is as if this is the only—we need that—I mean, yes, the part outside of the border adjustment tax is great. If we cannot pass this, we go to something smaller. We will get a lot of growth from it, especially on the corporation tax. I mean, I would love to see reforms on the individuals' side and reduction of rates, but this is not a priority. The corporation tax side—I mean, our system is absolutely awful. It is anti-competition. We have the highest rate of all the Organisation for Economic Co-operation and Development (OECD) countries. We have a worldwide tax system. This needs to happen, and a lot of growth will come from this. But, yes, the math does not work.

On this, you also bring some spending cuts to the table, which the plan does not address at all.

Senator PETERS. Thank you. Mr. Walker.

Mr. WALKER. It should be deficit-neutral, and one of the real questions would be is whether and to what extent you consider economic growth in calculating that as to whether or not it is deficit-neutral.

With regard to Social Security, coming back to that real quick, keep in mind two things about 1983. They had no choice but to reach an agreement in 1983 because the trust fund was going to zero within a matter of months. If it went to zero, tens of millions of people would have their checks cut. That was not politically feasible or acceptable. They had no choice.

But second, when they made the reforms in 1983, they did not consider known demographic trends. They only achieved actuarial balance over 75 years. They forgot that we have gone from 16 to 1 people working to retired to three to one, going to two to one by 2035. Next time you reform Social Security, you have to recognize demographic realities, demographics or destiny.

And last, what we tested for Social Security reform—again, not advocating that this is necessarily the right answer, but what got 77 percent support for Social Security reform of a demographically representative group of voters was the following: Raise but not eliminate the cap, considering 90 percent of taxable wages, which is what Reagan did back in the 80s.

Mr. ZANDI. Seventy percent, did you say?

Mr. WALKER. Ninety percent of taxable——

Mr. ZANDI. No, but the support was 70 percent?

Mr. WALKER. Seventy-seven percent for a package. Now, you have to keep in mind—and that is how you have to do it. If you do individual things, forget it. You are not going to get people to come together. You have to vote on packages. All right?

Raise the cap. Gradually raise the retirement age two years over 20 to 30 years, but provide an exception for certain occupations where they are not white collar occupations. You have to do that. You have to recognize that reality. Make the benefits more progressive. So give a higher replacement rate to people near the poverty level, a somewhat lower replacement rate for people that are higher income, but do not fully means-test it to make it a welfare program, and then consider going to an alternative form of CPI. Those got 77 percent support, which is even good enough in the Senate, I think.

Mr. ZANDI. Can I make one point about corporate tax reform that is going to be relevant to the debate, I think? I think it would be a mistake to try to get around the budget rules by sunsetting any tax proposal after a 10-year budget window, that particularly with regard to growth, if we go to corporate tax reform and the idea here is to promote growth, if in fact you sunset it after 10 years just to make it work from a reconciliation perspective, that will—because back to the policy uncertainty—significantly reduce the economic value of that kind of proposal. You are not accomplishing what you need to approach. In my view, that would be an error to go down that path. If you are going to do it, you have to do it in an honest way.

Senator PAUL. Well, I want to thank the panel for coming. I think we have had a good discussion, and I hope this is a beginning. I wish we had sort of a standing committee that was actually looking at entitlements. If I were in charge, there would be a committee looking at Social Security and Medicare and saying, "How do we come together?" And it would be a permanent committee, and it would be the most important committee around here. And we would devote time and resources day in and day out. And I think we could. I think we eventually could come to some arrangement. The idea that it is harder for people to do physical work, that there may be some accommodation, sure. I am sure we could find an agreement there. Does the age have to go up, though? The age has to go up. It is an enormous part of how you fix cost.

Two-thirds of the Social Security shortfall can be wiped out by raising the age. Can you have some exceptions for people who are not able to work as long? You could. But there are all kinds of things.

Which is worse? Raising taxes on everybody or means testing, or are they kind of the same thing? They are kind of the same thing. We could figure out how to do this, but we are not having the discussion.

So I was pleased with the discussion today. This is a beginning. I appreciate you taking your time to come in, and thank you, Senator Peters, for being part of it.

[Whereupon, at 3:59 p.m., the Subcommittee was adjourned.]

APPENDIX

———————

Opening Statement of Chairman Paul
FSO Subcommittee Hearing: *The Effect of Borrowing on Federal Spending*
March 29, 2017

I call this hearing of the Federal Spending Oversight Subcommittee to order.

Two weeks ago today, the federal government reached its credit limit.   As a nation, we owe almost $20 trillion, which is about $60,000 for each American alive today, including children.

Yet, we are told $20 trillion is not enough, that sometime soon Congress will be asked to increase our borrowing limit yet again.

That is what we want to explore here today. What is our debt situation, how it impacts our budget, and how should we respond?

Some argue raising the debt limit should be a routine vote; that any debate or amendment suggests the possibility of default and that is dangerous. I do not want to default, but I think it is proper for Congress to periodically approve more borrowing and not without making necessary reforms.

I also want to note, that on a monthly average cash flow basis, the federal government would be able to pay interest on the debt, salaries for our troops, social security, and much more. In fact, on an annualized basis we can fund 86 percent of the government without net borrowing. So, default is not necessarily unavoidable if the debt limit is not raised.

Some scholars argue we shouldn't worry; we don't really need to ever pay back our debt. Keynes said not to worry about the long run because in the end we'll all be dead; other have argued debt can be stabilized or simply inflated away.

I don't share these view, but even for those who do, the one thing we cannot outlive or inflate away is interest on the debt. This year alone, we will make $295 billion in interest payments. That is more than we will spend this year on seven cabinet departments, The White House, Congress, and the Courts, – COMBINED.

More concerning is how ongoing deficits mean interest will consume more and more of our budget in the years to come. I want to draw your attention to this chart; it shows the share of federal spending that goes to interest on the debt, discretionary spending, and mandatory spending over the next 30 years. That spans roughly a typical worker's career.

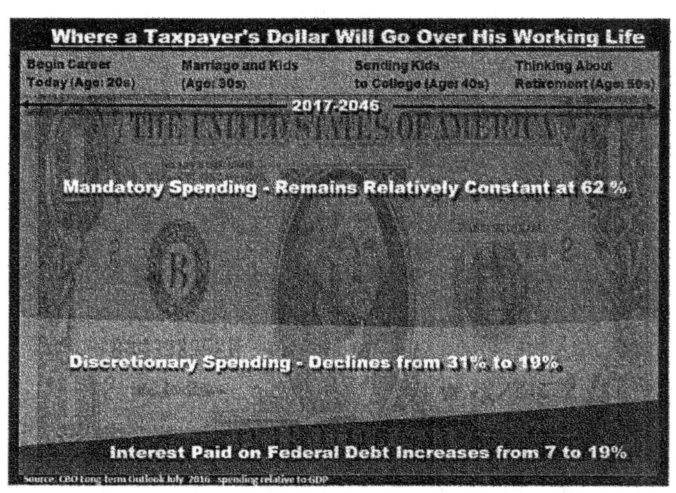

What we see is shocking. Today the American worker sees roughly 7 cents of their tax dollar go to interest and 30 cents to discretionary spending. But by the time a recent graduate today is near retirement, interest and discretionary spending will be taking an equal share of their tax dollar, roughly 19 cents each.

Of course these are ratios, we'll be spending more overall in 30 years; but the point is still clear, under the current course, interest will progressively squeeze out discretionary spending.

So, what do we get for interest, what are we trading defense and education spending for? Nothing, not one hour of work, not one sticky note.

We always hear spending today is an investment, or that cutting anything is too devastating. We hear that from both the right and the left, and we're always told we'll be fiscally responsible tomorrow.

What kind of investment is that? The reality is, tomorrow we won't have a choice, there will be cuts. When Congress spends money it does not have today, it means in the near future, we will be less safe and less educated. Not for children and grandchildren, but for people – adults - in the workforce today.

We simply cannot continue to keep racking up debt. Yet, just two months ago I proposed a budget that balanced in 5 years without touching Social Security and without an actual spending cut. Yet only 14 senators had the courage to vote for that budget.

So that brings me to my last point. Doing the right thing is hard and often not politically expedient.

Congress rarely makes simple but unpleasant choices, which means we end up facing difficult and unavoidable, catastrophic problems. We only act when circumstances force us to.

That is why the debt limit is important. It is our internal credit limit, not that of our creditors. It is an opportunity to reassess our spending, and ask, "how did we get here, and what do we do?"

Answering those questions as part of past debt limit debates have spawned most, if not all major federal fiscal process reforms. The most notable example is 1974 Budget Act, which came to be as the result of the 1972 debt limit debate. That act created procedures, road blocks, intended to prevent fiscal peril.

The '74 Act has its flaws; big spenders have had over 40 years to figure out how to beat it. The Budget Act was born during a debt ceiling debate. My hope, as we once again debate raising the debt ceiling, is that we reform spending at the same time.

With that, I'll recognize Ranking Member Peters for his opening statement. But, before I do, I just want to note this is Senator Peter's first hearing as Ranking Member of this subcommittee, so I'd like to welcome him and look forward to working with you. Senator Peters.

I want to first thank the Chairman, Senator Paul, for bringing us here to discuss the critical topic of the national debt, and the pressing matter of the debt ceiling.

I'd like to also give a sincere "thank you" to our distinguished panel of guests. Your perspectives of both the national debt and the debt ceiling are critical for us as policy makers.

Today we will consider what I see as two very significant, distinct, and most importantly, SOLVEABLE problems.

Perhaps I am an optimist, but finding sustainable solutions for our nation's debt, as well as finding a path forward on the debt ceiling, are both problems that can and should be solved in a responsible, bipartisan manner.

To me, working in a bipartisan manner on these issues is the only path forward – it is what I believe we were sent here to do – to find the solutions that put America on a path towards a sustainable fiscal future.

As 2017 progresses, we are going to hear many "School House Rocks" explanations of the debt limit, the statutory – and arbitrary – constraint on the amount of money the US Treasury can borrow.

Much of the conversation will be focused on questions like – when is the right time to talk about solutions for the long term debt and deficits?

We should be constantly working toward fiscal responsibility. This is not and should not be a seasonal debate. I'm sure the Chairman shares this sentiment.

But just as we should be constantly engaged in discussions about how to solve our long term issues, it is wholly irresponsible to turn this debate into one that threatens the full faith and credit of the United States.

The global economy relies on the fact that at the end of the day, no matter the chaos in the rest of the world, the United States Government will fulfill its obligations and pay its bills.

On March 16, 2017, under the Bipartisan Budget Act of 2015, the previously suspended debt ceiling was reinstated at just over $18 trillion.

Immediately on March 16, Treasury Secretary Mnuchin wrote to Congress to inform us that the United States Treasury was taking "extraordinary measures" to avoid a breach in the debt ceiling.

According to analysis of the debt limit conducted by both the Congressional Budget Office and the Bipartisan Policy Center, the Treasury Department's extraordinary measures may be able to extend the date to which the U.S. Government can fulfill its financial obligations into fall 2017, perhaps October or November.

However, Congress can, and should, immediately begin discussions to address our obligations. After having been through numerous debates on the debt limit since 2011, it would be the height of irresponsibility to let this debate slip into the midnight hour.

I remind my colleagues – while a breach of the debt ceiling would have unprecedented and potentially catastrophic impact on the global economy – brinksmanship alone has the potential to hurt everyday working families.

In 2011, as Congress struggled to reach an agreement at the last minute, the US debt was downgraded, consumer confidence fell sharply, and the stock market and credit markets took months to fully stabilize.

To some, the debate in Washington may seem abstract, but if we yet again engage in brinksmanship, we are jeopardizing the chance for a working-class family to purchase their first home, or to take out a loan to buy a much-needed car. And we are risking thousands of Americans' retirement savings that they have built up over a lifetime of hard work. This is not acceptable.

If there is to be a negotiation on the debt ceiling, I ask my colleagues, let it happen now. We cannot afford to let our differences risk the financial futures of American families.

Failure to act is also not an option when it comes to long term debt and deficit reduction.

Solving this challenge will take bipartisan cooperation – and it will require a comprehensive approach that addresses all three fundamental factors of deficit reduction: cutting spending, reforming taxes, and investing in economic growth.

Budget plans that shift the burden onto one group at the expense of another, or that ignore any of these basic factors, will not solve the problem.

We need to support economic growth, we need to find REAL solutions to curbing long term health care costs, we need to reform our tax code into one that promotes job creation and investment here at home in America, we need to make government more efficient, and we need to find RESPONSIBLE ways to cut spending.

I hope today serves as an open forum on these issues, both our long term debt as well as the debt limit. I know that each of our witnesses is well informed and highly respected on these topics.

Please use this forum to give us your honest assessment of these challenges. We may not agree on the proposals that we hear today, but it is only by engaging in a bipartisan, collaborative fashion that we are going to find the solutions that America deserves.

Thank you.

I applaud Subcommittee Chairman Paul for hosting this hearing to examine the effects of debt on federal spending. I would like to highlight the importance of transparency and honesty in the federal budget process. Accurate accounting for budgetary estimates is foundational to the integrity of the budget process. However, budgetary scoring conventions used by both the Congressional Budget Office (CBO) and the Joint Committee on Taxation (JCT), the organizations tasked with providing official budgetary and revenue scores, do not always reflect the economic reality. The treatment of interest costs represents one such departure from accurate budgetary scoring because financing costs are not considered when calculating the total cost of legislative proposals. As a result, CBO and JCT revenue scores often underestimate costs, causing inflated actual spending outlays after costly legislative measures are passed.

Interest costs are not a small part of the federal budget. In fact, net interest payments on the nation's debt alone are expected to be $768 billion by 2027, significantly above defense spending. Additionally, the Federal Reserve is highly anticipated to continue to raise interest rates by 0.25 percent increments, most recently increasing on March 15, 2017 only increasing the impact of interest costs. With CBO's projected FY17 deficit of $559B, this quarter percent increase alone amounts to about $1.4B in unaccounted for deficit spending in legislative proposal revenue estimates.

But there is a solution. Today, I introduced the Budgetary Accuracy in Scoring Interest Costs (BASIC) Act to require both CBO and JCT to include projected interest expense associated with legislative proposals in order to accurately account for budgetary costs. Such a change will reduce variances between budget costs and actual costs, creating clarity in the fiscal budgeting process to both legislators and the public.

United States Senate

Committee on Homeland Security and Governmental Affairs

Federal Spending Oversight and Emergency Management Sub-Committee

Hearing on "The Effect of Borrowing on Federal Spending"

March 29, 2017

Washington, DC

By: Hon. David M. Walker

Chairman Paul, Ranking Member Peters, and other members of the Sub-Committee, thank you for the opportunity to testify today on this important topic. I am currently a Senior Strategic Advisor with PwC Public Sector. I am also a member of a number of Governing Boards and Advisory Committees. However, today I am testifying as a private citizen and the immediate former Comptroller General of the United States.

The title of this hearing is: The effect of Borrowing on Federal Spending. The short answer is there are several implications of our current federal spending and borrowing practices. They include:

> o. Additional debt results in higher interest costs that can serve to crowd out other federal spending, especially discretionary spending, and/or increase pressure for tax increases.

> o. The Congressional Budget Office (CBO) has projected that interest costs will be the fastest growing expense in the federal budget on a percentage basis over the next 10-years. And what do we get for interest? Nothing!

> o. Excessive levels of debt as a percentage of the economy (GDP) can serve to reduce economic growth and job opportunities. It can also cause a "crisis of confidence' in the U.S. dollar and much higher interest rates if the market ever decides that the federal government has lost control of its finances and is not willing or able to regain control over them.

o. Additional debt serves to mortgage the future of our children, grandchildren and future generations at a time when they will face increasing competition in a much more interconnected and competitive global marketplace.

From a broader perspective, the United States has strayed from many of the key principles and values that it was founded on and which made us great. The federal government has also grown too big, promised too much, and needs to enact a variety of reforms in order to help create a better future for our country and its citizens. The balance of my statement will provide some background and ideas regarding these matters.

The United States was founded based on certain basic principles and values. These include, but are not limited to: individual liberty and opportunity, personal responsibility and accountability, limited but effective government, rule of law and equal justice under the law, fiscal responsibility, intergenerational equity and stewardship. Stewardship requires that leaders not just deliver positive results today, not just leave things better off when they leave than when they came, but also leave things better positioned for the future. This is consistent with the long-standing American value of doing everything possible to provide each generation with more opportunity and a better standing of living than the past. This important tradition is now at significant risk.

For many generations the United States was disciplined about federal spending and focused on the express roles allocated to the federal government under the U.S. Constitution. However, in 1913 three things happened that served to significantly increase the size and scope of the federal government and undercut state's rights. Specifically: adoption of a federal income tax; creation of the Federal Reserve, and; direct election of the U.S. Senators rather than have them appointed by State legislatures.

Since 1913 the federal government has grown from 2% of the nation's economy to about 21% today and increasing. Stated differently, the federal government is over 10 times larger today on a relative basis than in 1913 and it's still growing. In addition, in 1913 the Congress controlled 97% of all federal spending annually. The only thing that Congress did not control was interest expense. Today, in Fiscal 2016, 69% of federal spending was deemed to be "mandatory spending" (See Exhibit A). Shockingly, the 31%

of federal spending that was controlled included all of the express and enumerated responsibilities outlined for the federal government under the Constitution, and all investments in our future.

Discretionary spending is coming under increasing pressure since mandatory spending is increasing at rates faster than the economy due to known demographic trends and rising health care costs. The bottom line is, Congress has lost control of the budget, our debt burdens are escalating to imprudent levels, and our collective future is now "at risk".

The federal government is still adding debt faster than the growth rate of the economy and interest rates have started to rise. The Congressional Budget Office (CBO) now estimates that interest expense will be the fastest growing category of spending growth as a percentage of the budget over the next 10-years. A recent independent analysis by Brian Riedl of the Manhattan Institute showed that if interest rates were to return the average rates in the 1990s that, the 2027 projected budget deficit would increase from $1.4 trillion to $2.2 trillion.

Speaking of interest rates, the Federal Reserve has only recently begun to increase its discount rate. The Fed still has trillions of U.S. Government debt that it needs to dispose of. Social Security is now in a negative versus positive cash flow position since interest credits are a non cash item. In addition, the appetite for foreign government investment in U.S. Government debt is declining for a variety of reasons. All of these factors will serve to put upward pressure on interest rates over time, especially if the economy starts to grow at a more brisk rate.

Since the beginning of our republic, there have only been two times in our nation's history that federal public debt as a percentage of the economy (GDP) exceeded 40%. Those two times during the later part and in the immediate aftermath of World War II and in the 21st Century, including today. After World War II, the U.S. was over 50% of global GDP, there were over 16 persons working for every person drawing Social Security benefits and the dollar was a good as gold. U.S. brought back fiscal responsibility and took a range of steps to grow the economy much faster than the nation's public debt. The result was a dramatic reduction in federal public debt/GDP from over 100% of GDP to less than 40% by 1980. Today, federal debt held by the public is approaching 80% of GDP and, based on estimates by the Government Accountability Office (GAO), the percentage of debt held by the public/GDP is on a path to rise to levels far in excess of the nation's historical high absent a major course correction (See Exhibit B).

Today the U.S. represents about 24% of global GDP, there are about 3.1 persons working for every person on Social Security and the dollar is not backed by gold. Current trends are not positive in any of these areas.

Defusing our nation's ticking debt bomb will require an unprecedented public education and engagement effort as a prelude to major budget, tax, Social Security, Medicare/Medicare, health care, defense, government organization/operations, and political reforms. I led a 27 state effort in the fall of 2012 to test how such an effort could be conducted and whether it would serve as an effective means to bring Americans together to achieve a common goal (i.e., reducing public debt/GDP to a stated level by a specified date) and in a manner that was consistent with stated principles and values that could achieve a super-majority support and served to bring people together than rather than divide people apart.

The result of the above effort proved that achieving the needed comprehensive reforms is possible. For example, 77% to over 90% of representative groups of voters in Ohio and Virginia, both so-called "swing states, agreed on a range of reforms in all of the above referenced areas that would result in public debt/GDP being reduced to 60% by 2030 in installments and in a manner that would be sustainable over time. I would be happy to answer any questions about this effort should you so desire.

The primary mechanism that Congress has used to control the level of federal debt in the past is the debt ceiling limit. While this mechanism in only direct debt speed brake the Congress has, it has not proven to be effective in limiting the growth of federal debt, forcing a reconsideration of proper role of the federal government, including the need to reform mandatory spending programs and tax expenditures. In fact, total federal debt subject to the debt ceiling limit will soon pass $20,000,000,000,000. This is about 105% of GDP and about 3.5 times what the same number was in 2000! Clearly, the federal government has lost control of its finances.

Arguably, 2003 was the year that the federal government lost its way. In that year alone, the federal government passed a second round of debt financed tax cuts, invaded a sovereign nation without declaring war and charging the cost to the nation's credit card, and expanded Medicare to add prescription drugs. The latter action added over $9 trillion in new unfunded obligations when Medicare was already underfunded by over $19 trillion! And this occurred just three short years after the then Chairman of the Federal Reserve testified that he was concerned that the federal government might pay off all the federal debt. A concern that I did not share and testified accordingly at the time. One thing is clear, we don't have to worry about that anymore.

In my view, given recent history, the debt ceiling limit needs to be replaced with stronger statutory budget controls and a Constitutional amendment that would limit public debt/GDP with specific targets and automatic enforcement mechanisms if the targets are not met. In my view, a debt/GDP fiscal responsibility approach is vastly superior to a "balanced budget" approach. I am happy to discuss why and a related illustrative amendment, should you so desire.

As you may be aware, there is currently an effort underway to achieve a state led Convention under Article V of the Constitution to restore fiscal responsibility at the federal level. Twenty eight of the required 34 states have already passed related resolutions and several groups are working to make this concept a reality. One of these groups is called the Balanced Budget Amendment Task Force. Michigan is one of the 28 states that has passed a related fiscal responsibility resolution but Kentucky has yet to do so. Hopefully the Kentucky legislature will do so either this year or next.

Speaking of states, I lead an annual effort to rank the 50 states based on their relative financial position, competitive posture and migration patterns. This report reveals a wide disparity among the states. It also serves to demonstrate that cash-based "balanced budget" amendments have not proven to be effective mechanisms to ensure fiscal prudence and sustainability at the state level. As an example, both Kentucky and Michigan are required to have "balanced budgets". However, both states face fiscal sustainability challenges of differing degrees of magnitude due, in large part, to underfunded retirement plans. Kentucky is ranked number 49 and Michigan number 41 out of the 50 states in relative financial position, with number 50 (i.e., New Jersey) being the worst state (See Exhibit C).

States need to take steps to improve their competitive posture and put their finances in order. After all, eventually the federal government will take steps to restructure its finances, and when it does, the downdraft will have an adverse impact on troubled states. In addition, while the federal government can create money and manipulate interest rates, state governments can't. And while municipalities can file for bankruptcy, states can't. Furthermore, most Americans do not want to leave the United States; however, most do not have a problem leaving a state, especially when they retire.

In summary, we live in a great nation but we have strayed from the principles and values that made us great. We are currently on an imprudent and unsustainable fiscal path. We need to be honest with ourselves and the American people. Tough choices are required on the spending and revenue side of the budget in order to restore fiscal responsibility, enhance economic growth, and create a better future. The sooner we start making those choices the better so the miracle of compounding can start working for us rather than against us as it is now.

Thank you again for the opportunity to testify. I would be happy to answer any questions that members of the sub-committee may have.

U.S. Budget Outlays FY 2016
Total $3.919 Trillion
Source: Cong Budget Office

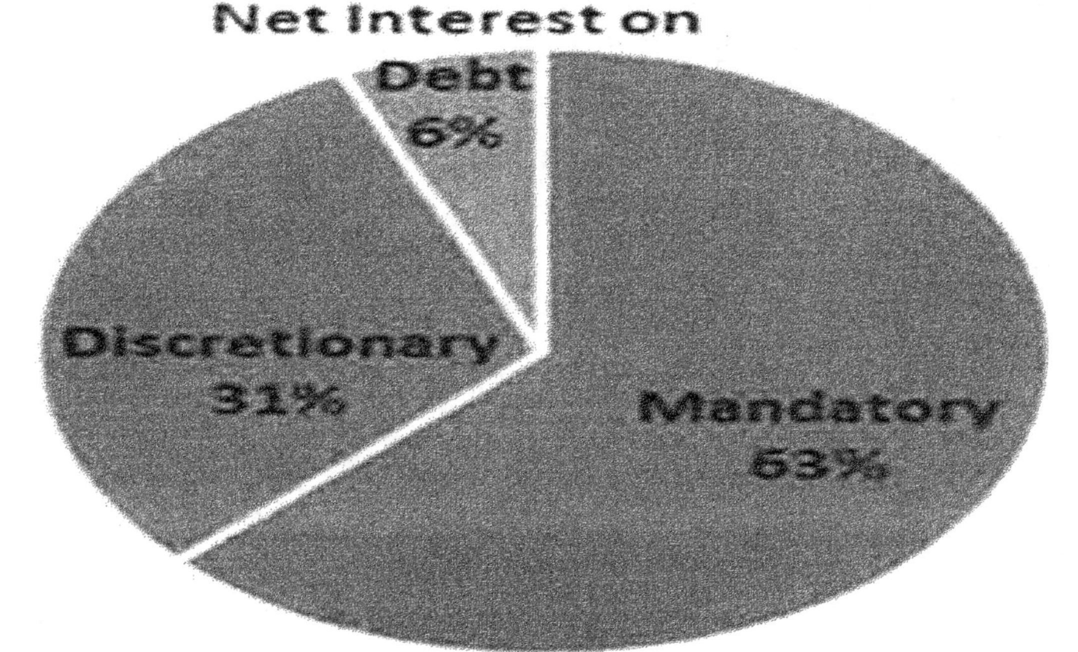

Federal Debt Held by the Public as a Share of GDP (Exhibit B)

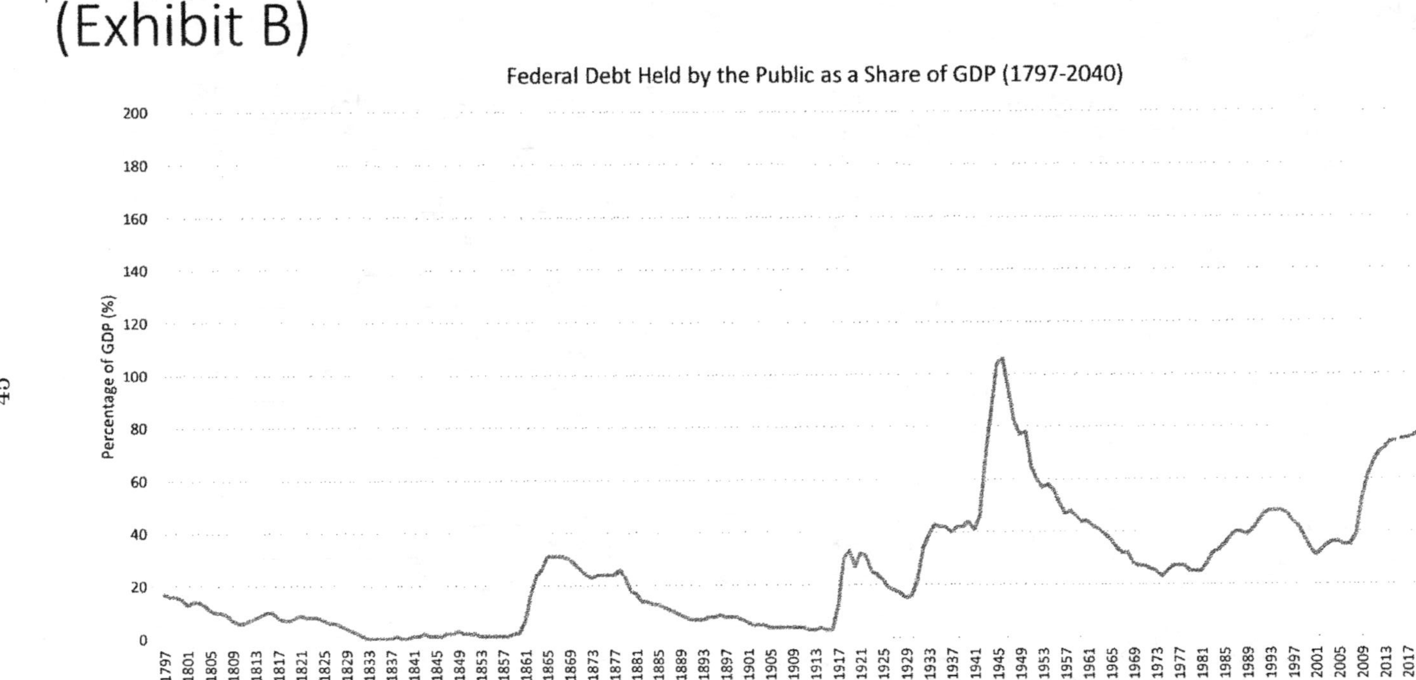

Source: Government Accountability Office, 2015.

Relative Financial Position and Competitiveness by State (Exhibit C)

#	State	%		#	State	%		#	State	%
1.	Alaska (5)	70.0%		18.	Missouri (3)	5.9%		35.	Pennsylvania (4)	25.7%
2.	North Dakota (2)	49.5%		18.	Oklahoma (3)	5.9%		36.	Vermont (5)	28.9%
3.	Wyoming (3)	43.3%		20.	Colorado (1)	6.0%		37.	Mississippi (5)	29.5%
4.	Utah (1)	7.2%		21.	Arizona (2)	6.1%		38.	Alabama* (4)	30.1%
5.	South Dakota (2)	6.0%		22.	Nevada (3)	7.1%		39.	West Virginia (5)	32.5%
6.	Nebraska (2)	5.8%		22.	New Hampshire (4)	7.1%		40.	California (4)	32.8%
7.	New Mexico (4)	5.3%		24.	Georgia (1)	7.7%		41.	Michigan (3)	33.6%
8.	Idaho (2)	4.6%		25.	Wisconsin (2)	8.3%		42.	Delaware (3)	34.1%
9.	Tennessee (1)	4.4%		26.	Ohio (2)	9.4%		43.	New York (4)	34.7%
10.	Iowa (1)	1.8%		27.	Kansas (3)	11.8%		44.	Louisiana (5)	37.9%
11.	Oregon (3)	0.7%		28.	Texas (1)	13.6%		45.	Hawaii (5)	44.2%
12.	Florida (1)	2.3%		29.	North Carolina (1)	15.2%		46.	Massachusetts (3)	44.7%
13.	Virginia (1)	2.4%		30.	Washington (2)	15.5%		47.	Connecticut (5)	67.2%
14.	Minnesota (2)	2.6%		31.	Maine (5)	16.5%		48.	Illinois (4)	75.3%
15.	Montana (3)	2.9%		32.	Maryland (4)	20.1%		49.	Kentucky (4)	79.5%
16.	Arkansas (4)	3.3%		33.	South Carolina (2)	21.8%		50.	New Jersey (5)	86.9%
17.	Indiana (1)	4.6%		34.	Rhode Island (5)	25.5%				

Completed: January 2017

Rankings are based on Fiscal 2015 CAFR financial data and the latest migration and competitiveness data for 2016

*Alabama Fiscal Year 2015 CAFR had not yet been released. Fiscal Year 2014 CAFR data is used here instead.

- State names in black denote positive state migration, state names in red denote negative state migration for the period 7/1/15-6/30/16
- Percentages in red denote an accumulated burden per taxpayer as a percentage of median household income, percentages in black denote an accumulated surplus per taxpayer as a percentage of household income
- Relative Competitive Posture in 2016 By Quintile – (1), (2), (3), (4) and (5)
- Sources: Truth in Accounting's State Data Lab, U.S. Census Bureau, Forbes, CEO Magazine, and CNBC
- The initial and full PwC State Financial Position Index (SFPI) and Competitiveness Report that used 2014 CAFR and 2015 competitiveness and migration data can be found at http://pwc.to/1O6S85f This report contains explanations of key terms and computations.

MERCATUS CENTER
George Mason University

Change the Trajectory of Debt

Veronique de Rugy
Senior Research Fellow, Mercatus Center at George Mason University

March 29th, 2017

Senate Committee on Homeland Security and Governmental Affairs, Subcommittee on
Federal Spending Oversight and Emergency Management
Hearing: The Effect of Borrowing on Federal Spending

Chairman Paul, Ranking Member Peters, and members of the subcommittee:

Thank you for the opportunity to testify today.

After briefly looking at how we arrived where we presently are, I would like to make the
following points:

1) High and increasing debt has adverse consequences for our economy.
2) At the minimum, Congress should look for institutional reforms (such as credible
   budget caps and a BRAC commission for discretionary spending) that would be a
   first step to addressing our long-term debt problem as a condition to raising the debt
   ceiling.
3) Optimally, Congress would reform the drivers of our future debt as it raises the debt
   ceiling, ending a cycle of pushing the unsustainability of the federal government,
   punishing taxes, and slower growth onto future generations.
4) There are a few measures the Department of the Treasury can take, and there are
   sufficient assets available to prevent a default for several months, which should give
   Congress and the administration some time to reach an agreement that reflects the
   commitment to implement reform.

THE INCREASING FEDERAL DEBT

The origins of the federal government's statutory debt limit can be traced back to 1917, when
the country was borrowing money to finance the First World War.[1] Limitations on federal
borrowing were intended to control congressional spending by limiting the amount of debt
that the federal government could accumulate. Policymakers have routinely pushed the
debt limit ever higher with the passage of time. Indeed, the limit has been increased almost

---

[1] D. Andrew Austin, "The Debt Limit: History and Recent Increases," Congressional Research Service, October
1, 2015, 5.

3434 Washington Blvd., 4th Floor, Arlington, VA 22201   Phone: (703) 993-4930   Fax: (703) 993-4935   www.mercatus.org

21 times between 1993 and 2015,[2] including the Bipartisan Budget Act of 2015 passed in October 2015 that suspended the debt limit until March 15, 2017.[3] During that time, the federal debt ballooned from less than $5 trillion in 1993 to $19.9 trillion as of February 2017.[4]

As of March 16 of this year, a new debt limit has been established to reflect the additional borrowing that took place during the suspension and through March 15, 2017. From this point on, "Treasury will, from that date forward, have no room to borrow under standard operating procedures. Therefore, to avoid breaching the ceiling, the Treasury would begin taking the extraordinary measures that would allow it to continue to borrow for a limited time," according to the Congressional Budget Office (CBO).[5]

It is worth noting that the 2015 suspension of the debt limit was part of a deal to increase spending (for the second time) above what was intended by caps implemented by the Budget Control Act of 2011. Despite the popular perception of Republicans and Democrats caught in gridlock, the truth is that after the political dust settles, the end result is always the same: a bipartisan agreement on more spending and more debt.

This needs to change. According to the most recent ten-year fiscal forecast from the Congressional Budget Office, federal outlays remain near 21 percent of GDP for the next few years—higher than their average of 20.2 percent over the past 50 years. Also, if current laws generally remained the same, growth in outlays would outstrip growth in the economy, and outlays would rise to 23.4 percent of GDP by 2027.

CBO projections also show that federal debt held by the public will reach 77.5 percent by the end of 2017. It is expected to grow from $14.8 trillion this year to $24.8 trillion by 2027. Gross debt will reach $20.3 trillion at the end of this year and total $27.5 trillion at the end of 2027.

That's probably an underestimate, since it is a projection based on the assumption that promises to cut spending and raise taxes will be kept. Based on Congress's termination of the sequester years ahead of schedule and its historical propensity to spend more and more each year, this is unlikely. The projections also assume that the economy will grow at current projected rates and without any recessions. This too is unlikely, because the economy, historically, has cycled into recession every five to six years.

Deficits are projected to balloon from $559 billion in 2017 to $1.4 trillion in 2027. Over the coming decade, the size of the federal deficit will double to reach an almost annual gap of 5 percent of GDP in 2027. CBO predicts that cumulative deficits will total $10 trillion between this year and 2027.

---

[2] D. Andrew Austin, "The Debt Limit Since 2011," Congressional Research Service, March 14, 2017, 5.

[3] Veronique de Rugy, "Budget Deal Is Business-as-Usual in Washington," Mercatus Center at George Mason University, November 18, 2015.

[4] Department of the Treasury, "Monthly Statement of the Public Debt of the United States, February 28, 2017," table I—Summary of Treasury Securities Outstanding.

[5] Congressional Budget Office, "Federal Debt and the Statutory Limit, March 2017," March 7, 2017.

The projected explosion of spending from programs such as Social Security, Medicare, and Medicaid will trigger even higher levels of debt in the years outside the 10-year budget window.

The growth in spending on mandatory programs—such as Medicare, Medicaid, Affordable Care Act subsidies, and Social Security—is the driving force behind this spending growth and our exploding debt. In 2017, spending on those programs will reach $2.1 trillion, or 54 percent of total spending.

Unfortunately, as the debt grows, so too will the interest payments on that debt. Debt payments, which were $270 billion in 2017, are currently projected to increase to $768 billion in 2027. If the United States doesn't change course, debt will end up as one of the federal government's biggest budget items. Our unfunded liabilities keep going up, too. The net present value of the promises made to the American people that the United States does not have the money to pay is roughly $75.5 trillion, according to the Treasury Department.

Even leaving aside the fact that the federal budget isn't sustainable on its current trajectory, high debt levels are problematic. As CBO explained a few years ago:

> Such high and rising debt later in the coming decade would have serious negative consequences: When interest rates return to higher (more typical) levels, federal spending on interest payments would increase substantially. Moreover, because federal borrowing reduces national saving, over time the capital stock would be smaller and total wages would be lower than they would be if the debt was reduced. In addition, lawmakers would have less flexibility than they would have if debt levels were lower to use tax and spending policy to respond to unexpected challenges. Finally, a large debt increases the risk of a fiscal crisis, during which investors would lose so much confidence in the government's ability to manage its budget that the government would be unable to borrow at affordable rates.[6]

These numbers should be at the forefront in any discussion about the need to raise the debt ceiling again.

WHAT'S AT STAKE

The debt ceiling will need to be raised in the near future. As such, we can expect Washington to have the same debate it has had for the last few years about whether or not to raise the debt ceiling and under what circumstances. On one side, you will find those who want to raise the limit with no conditions. On the other side, you will find those who will demand reforms in exchange for yet another increase in the debt ceiling.

Default should not be an option on the table. However, raising the debt ceiling without a commitment to improve our long-term debt problem has adverse consequences. In 2011, the

---

[6] Congressional Budget Office, "Updated Budget Projections: Fiscal Years 2013 to 2023," May 2013.

rating agency Fitch Ratings warned the US government that while it wanted the debt ceiling to be raised, it also wanted the government to come up with a credible medium-term deficit-reduction plan.[7] Other rating agencies at the time also warned the United States of the negative consequences of not dealing with the country's long-term debt.

The federal budget is unsustainable. According to economist Paul Winfree, this unsustainability is driven by 2 percent of nearly 1,800 spending accounts funding all government activities—mainly public healthcare programs administered by the Department of Health and Human Services and benefits paid by the Social Security's Old-Age and Survivors Insurance Trust Fund.[8] The spending on those accounts is about 60 percent of gross spending over 10 years. It is currently projected to keep increasing faster than GDP, but this cannot sustainably continue indefinitely.

This makes it incredibly important to address our country's long term debt problem. A delay in dealing with this underlying unsustainability will severely restrict our future fiscal choices and make it very hard to respond to emergencies.

With that in mind, the need to raise the debt ceiling offers a great opportunity to demand that Congress take some steps toward a more fiscally responsible future. Optimally, the White House, Congress, and Treasury will raise the debt limit while Congress passes and the president signs a credible plan to reduce near-and long-term spending at the same time.

It takes some time to come up with such a plan. Fortunately, this administration acknowledges that the United States need not risk defaulting on its debt while it figures out what reforms can be adopted as part of a debt ceiling deal. The Treasury Department has the legal authority to use extraordinary measures to prioritize interest payments on the debt above all else, thus avoiding a default.

As was the case in 2011, the United States will have enough expected cash flow (tax revenue) and assets on hand to avoid either of these unattractive options. Managing payments in this manner is by no means optimal, and Treasury officials have indicated that this will be difficult owing to payment automation. That said, it is important to recognize the options that are available to prevent a default. While Washington has difficult choices to make, defaulting on its debt obligations is not one of them, such a step should not be a consideration in the current or foreseeable discussion about how to handle the debt limit or reduce long-term government spending.

---

[7] Veronique de Rugy, "Policy Implications of the S&P Warnings," *The Corner, National Review Online*, July 22, 2011. Also see Jeannette Neumann, "Fitch Unveils Two Possible Routes to Downgrading US Debt Rating," *Wall Street Journal*, January 15, 2013.

[8] Paul Winfree, "Causes of the Federal Government's Unsustainable Spending" (Backgrounder No. 3133, Heritage Foundation, Washington, DC, July 7, 2016).

REAL INSTITUTIONAL REFORM
We can predict that in the coming months the heated rhetoric about whether Congress should raise the debt ceiling will obscure the federal government's real problem: an unprecedented increase in government spending and the future explosion of entitlement spending has created a fiscal imbalance today and for the years to come. No matter what Congress decides to do about the debt ceiling, the United States must implement institutional reforms that constrain government spending and return it to a sustainable fiscal position.

Real institutional reforms, as opposed to one-time cuts, would change the trajectory of fiscal policy and put the United States on a more sustainable path. Such reforms could include:

1. **A constitutional amendment to limit spending.** The inability of lawmakers to constrain their own spending makes spending limits enforced through the US Constitution preferable.[9]

2. **Meaningful budget reforms that limit lawmakers' tendency to spend.** In the absence of constitutional rules, budget rules should have broad scope, few and high-hurdle escape clauses, and minimal accounting discretion.[10]

3. **The end of budget gimmicks.** Creative bookkeeping is at the center of many countries' financial troubles. Congress should end abuse of the emergency spending rule, reliance on overly rosy scenarios, and all other gimmicks and institute a transparent budget process.[11]

4. **A strict cut-as-you-go system.** This system should apply to the entire federal budget, not just to a small portion of it. There should be no new spending without offsetting cuts.[12]

5. **A BRAC-like commission for discretionary spending.** Commissions composed of independent experts often tackle intractable political problems successfully.[13]

REAL ENTITLEMENT REFORMS
Some members of Congress believe that we can stabilize our debt problems by raising taxes, preferably on the wealthiest Americans. However, the math doesn't add up. Other members believe that we can make the budget more sustainable by simply reducing nondefense discretionary spending, engaging in regulatory reforms, and cutting taxes. While there is

---

[9] David M. Primo, "Constitution is Only Way to Cut US Deficit," *Bloomberg*, February 24, 2011.

[10] David M. Primo, "Making Budget Rules Bite" (Mercatus on Policy, Mercatus Center at George Mason University, Arlington, VA, March 2010).

[11] Veronique de Rugy, "Budget Gimmicks or the Destructive Art of Creative Accounting" (Mercatus Working Paper, Mercatus Center at George Mason University, Arlington, VA, 2010).

[12] Veronique de Rugy and David Bieler, "Is PAYGO a No-Go?" (Mercatus on Policy, Mercatus Center at George Mason University, Arlington, VA, April 2010).

[13] Jerry Brito, "The BRAC Model for Spending Reform" (Mercatus on Policy, Mercatus Center at George Mason University, Arlington, VA, February 2010).

some merit to doing all these things, it won't be enough to address the unsustainability of our fiscal outlook.

As I mentioned earlier, the drivers of our future debt are spending on Medicare, Medicaid, and Social Security. Without reforms today, vast tax increases will be needed later to pay for the unfunded promises made to a steadily growing cohort of seniors. For instance, looking only at the excess spending growth in Medicare and Medicaid, Katherine Baicker and Jonathan Skinner find that "if spending growth is completely funded through tax increases, by 2060 GDP would be reduced by between 5 percent and 11 percent, depending on the future tax changes."[14]

While there is some disagreement among economists when it comes to fiscal policy prescriptions, a consensus has emerged recently that spending-based fiscal adjustments are not only more likely to reduce the debt-to-GDP ratio than tax-based ones, but they are also less likely to trigger a recession.[15] In fact, if accompanied by the right type of policies (especially changes to public employees' pay and public pension reforms), spending-based adjustments can actually be associated with economic growth.

Fortunately, numerous workable solutions are available to lawmakers, including adding a system of personal savings accounts to Social Security, liberalizing medical savings accounts, and making the latter permanent to reduce healthcare costs by increasing competition between providers and making consumers more responsive to tradeoffs.[16]

These options would encourage families to save more and use their money more responsibly, in a manner more consistent with their long-term needs. And because taxpayers remain in control of their wealth, they can bequeath any surplus to their heirs—giving the next generation a head start when it comes to building assets.

Better yet, we should free the healthcare supply from the many constraints imposed by federal and state governments and the special interests they serve.[17]

The stakes are high: Bringing revolutionary innovation to this industry could mean not just bending the healthcare cost curve but breaking it to bits—making the need for health insurance much less important if not moot in many cases.

---

[14] Winfree, "Causes of the Federal Government's Unsustainable Spending," 17.

[15] Veronique de Rugy, "The Effect of Tax Increases and Spending Cuts on Economic Growth" (Testimony before the Senate Budget Committee, Mercatus Center at George Mason University, Arlington, VA, May 22, 2013).

[16] Chris Edwards and Tad DeHaven, "War between the Generations: Federal Spending on the Elderly Set to Explode" (Policy Analysis No. 488, Cato Institute, Washington, DC, September 16, 2003).

[17] Robert Graboyes, *Fortress and Frontier in American Health Care* (Arlington, VA: Mercatus Center at George Mason University, 2014).

REVENUE AND ASSETS AVAILABLE TO FUND OUR COMMITMENT UNTIL AN AGREEMENT IS REACHED

When the government reaches the debt ceiling and the Treasury is no longer able to issue federal debt, the federal government could reduce spending, increase federal revenues by a corresponding amount to cover the gap, or find other funding mechanisms. This would allow time for Congress and the president to reach an agreement to make some important policy changes to change the debt trajectory we are on.

At that time, the Department of the Treasury will have several financial management options to continue paying the government's obligations. These include (1) prioritizing payments;[18] (2) taking financial steps, including permitting the suspension of investments in, and the redemption of securities held by, certain government trust funds or postponing the sale of nonmarketable debt;[19] (3) liquidating some assets to pay government bills;[20] and (4) using the Social Security Trust Fund to continue paying Social Security benefits.[21]

PRIORITIZING PAYMENTS

The secretary of the treasury has long-standing authority to prioritize payments and does not have to pay bills in the order in which they are received. The Government Accountability Office found that

> the Secretary of the Treasury has the authority to determine the order in which obligations are to be paid should the Congress fail to raise the statutory debt ceiling and revenues are inadequate to cover all required payments. There is no statute or other basis for concluding that the Treasury must pay outstanding obligations in the order they are presented for payment. Treasury is free to liquidate obligations in any order it determines will best serve the interests of the United States.[22]

According to a report by the Department of the Treasury's Inspector General (IG), during the 2011 debt ceiling crisis, the Treasury "considered a range of options with respect to how Treasury would operate if the debt ceiling was not raised." Further, the report notes that Treasury officials told the IG that "organizationally they viewed the option of delaying payments as the least harmful among the options under review" and that "the decision of

---

[18] Jason J. Fichtner and Veronique de Rugy, "The Debt Ceiling: What Is at Stake?" (Mercatus Research, Mercatus Center at George Mason University, Arlington, VA, 2011).

[19] Jason J. Fichtner and Veronique de Rugy, "The Debt Limit Debate" (Mercatus on Policy, Mercatus Center at George Mason University, Arlington, VA, May 2011).

[20] Fichtner and de Rugy, "The Debt Ceiling: What is at Stake?"

[21] The Social Security Trust Funds can only be used to pay Social Security benefits. See Glenn Kessler, "Can President Obama Keep Paying Social Security Benefits Even If the Debt Ceiling Is Reached?," *Washington Post*, July 13, 2011; Contract with America Advancement Act of 1996, Pub. L. No. 104-121, 110 Stat. 847 (1996).

[22] Government Accountability Office, letter to Senator Bob Packwood, October 9, 1985.

how Treasury would have operated if the U.S. had exhausted its borrowing authority would have been made by the President in consultation with the Secretary of the Treasury."[23]

TEMPORARY MEASURES

During the last debt ceiling debate in 2011, my colleague Jason Fichtner and I listed all the assets that Treasury could tap into to avoid a default until the president and Congress reached an agreement.[24] For instance, we found that Treasury was expected to collect $2.6 trillion in revenue. As we explained:

> That alone would be enough to cover interest on the debt ($218 billion), thereby avoiding any technical default of the US government on its debt obligations to Social Security ($809 billion), Medicare ($581 billion), and Medicaid ($267 billion), and it would leave approximately $725 billion for other priorities.

In addition, we noted that the Department of the Treasury had financial measures at its disposal to fund government operations temporarily without having to issue new debt. To be clear, our list was only meant to present the range of possible options available to Congress. And as we noted then, they may well be neither good nor desirable options. These assets totaled $1.9 trillion and included $50.2 billion in nonrestricted cash on hand,[25] $121.1 billion in restricted cash and other monetary assets (gold, international monetary assets, and foreign currency),[26] or the redemption of existing investments in other trust funds.[27]

We also noted that the government could rely on the determination of a "debt issuance suspension period." This determination would permit the redemption of existing, and the suspension of new, investments of the Civil Service Retirement and Disability Fund (CSRDF).[28] The latest data show $858.7 billion in intergovernmental holdings in the CSRDF.[29]

---

[23] Department of the Treasury, Office of Inspector General, letter to Senator Orrin G. Hatch, OIG-CA-12-006, August 24, 2012.

[24] Jason J. Fichtner and Veronique de Rugy, "The Debt Ceiling: Assets Available to Prevent Default" (Mercatus Research, Mercatus Center at George Mason University, Arlington, VA, 2013).

[25] Department of the Treasury, "Daily Treasury Statement," January 14, 2013.

[26] Department of the Treasury, "2012 Financial Report of the US Government," 2013, 65. Note: At the time, the Treasury owned approximately 261.4 million ounces of gold and marked the value of its gold holdings at $42 per ounce, giving a reported value of $11.1 billion. At a spot market price of $1,500 per ounce, Treasury's gold holdings could be valued near $400 billion.

[27] Department of the Treasury, "Monthly Statement of the Public Debt of the United States, December 31, 2015."

[28] In September 1985, the Treasury took the step of disinvesting the Civil Service Retirement and Disability Trust Fund, the Social Security Trust Funds, and several smaller trust funds.

[29] Office of Personnel Management, "Civil Service Retirement and Disability Fund Annual Report: Fiscal Year Ended September 30, 2015," January 2016.

Today, the numbers are different, but the same assets may be used to avoid a default, as confirmed by CBO.[30] Relying on any of these sources of funds or increasing the debt ceiling without reducing existing budget commitments illustrates the irresponsibility of the path the country is on and the urgent need for institutional spending reform. Nonetheless, these assets could be used as a temporary measure to allow Congress and the administration to negotiate spending reductions and institutional reforms to the budget process to ensure the nation is put back on a sound fiscal path.

Thank you. I am happy to take your questions.

---

[30] Congressional Budget Office, "Federal Debt and the Statutory Limit, March 2017."

Written Testimony of Mark Zandi
Chief Economist, Moody's Analytics

Before the Federal Spending Oversight and Emergency Management Subcommittee
of the Committee on Homeland Security and Governmental Affairs

"The Effect of Borrowing on Federal Spending"

March 29, 2017

Federal policymakers face a daunting number of significant pressing fiscal challenges. Most immediately, Congress has an April 28 deadline to renew expiring government spending authority through the end of the current fiscal year. Failure to do so could result in a government shutdown.

Then there is the budget for fiscal 2018, which is sure to be a matter of significant debate given President Trump's recent call for big increases in spending on the military and veterans' benefits, and commensurate cuts to nondefense discretionary programs.

The Treasury debt limit was also reinstated on March 16, although the Treasury probably has until at least August and perhaps as long as early October before it runs out of cash to pay bills coming due.

Policymakers appear likely to take up comprehensive tax reform this year. This will involve lowering marginal tax rates for businesses and individuals, and scaling back or eliminating preferences in the tax code to help pay for the lower rates. To pay for significant tax cuts, policymakers will need to find other sources of revenue or additional cuts in government spending, both of which will be extraordinarily difficult to do.

And then there is the nation's longer-run fiscal problems. The federal budget deficit is currently running at nearly $600 billion annually, equal to just over 3% of GDP. Publicly traded federal debt is equal to more than 75% of GDP, more than double what it was a decade ago, prior to the Great Recession. But more disconcerting, without significant changes to federal tax and spending policies, the federal government's deficits and debt load will steadily increase. The Congressional Budget Office estimates that by 2020, if no changes are made to current law, 92 cents of every federal tax dollar will go toward mandatory spending and interest. A decade from now this will rise to more than one dollar. This is not sustainable.

This written testimony will focus on the potential economic impact of political brinkmanship over increasing the Treasury debt limit. Such brinkmanship would be very costly to taxpayers, and under some scenarios catastrophic for the economy. This testimony will also provide a few suggestions policymakers may want to consider to address the nation's looming problem with deficits and debt.

Treasury debt limit countdown

In a letter to House Speaker Paul Ryan, Treasury Secretary Steve Mnuchin confirmed that the Treasury debt limit, which was suspended by the Bipartisan Budget Act of 2015, would be reinstated on March 16 and that he would start undertaking extraordinary measures to preserve the Treasury's cash to avoid defaulting on its obligations.

The Treasury looks to run out of room under the $19.9 trillion debt ceiling as soon as August, but no later than early October. Under the most likely scenario, the Treasury will be able to manage until the September 15 corporate tax deadline, when an inflow of tax receipts will provide another couple of weeks' worth of headroom under the limit. However, Congress will need to raise the limit by October 5 (see Chart 1).[1]

Chart 1: Oct. 5 Is Debt Ceiling Point of No Return

Estimated borrowing capacity under reinstated debt limit, $ bil

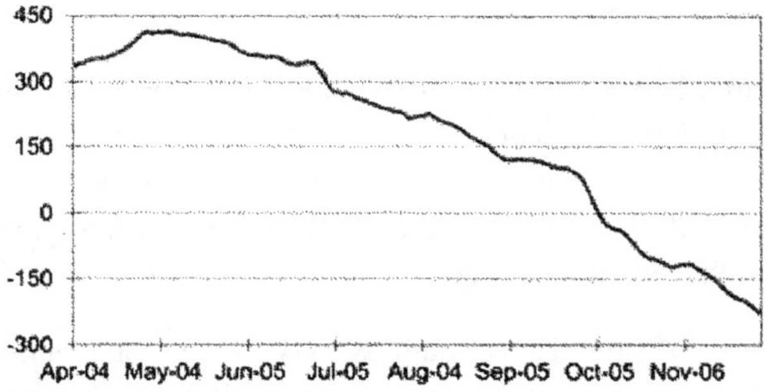

Sources: Treasury, Moody's Analytics

Any thought that Treasury would be able to pay holders of U.S. government securities first, and thus avoid defaulting on its obligation, is misplaced. Treasury has the technical ability to pay bond investors before others, as those payments are handled by a different computer system than other government obligations, but the Treasury believes it is not legally viable to do so, and politically it would be very difficult to pay bond investors before, say, Social Security recipients.

Even if the Treasury did pay bond investors first, this would not stop investors from demanding a much higher interest rate for the legal uncertainty and the real possibility that they may not get paid on time in the future. Bond investors, especially those overseas, would reasonably ask whether Congress would actually allow them to be paid ahead of American seniors.

Deciding which other bills receive priority would be all but impossible, as the Treasury could not sort through the blizzard of payments due each day. More likely, the Treasury would delay all payments until it received enough cash to pay a specific day's bills, as outlined in a 2012 report by Treasury's inspector general.

The Federal Reserve could restart quantitative easing—purchases of Treasury bonds—but any benefits would likely be overwhelmed as global investors sold U.S. securities. Financial markets would surely be spooked. Sometime in early October, there would be a TARP moment, harkening back to that day in autumn 2008 when Congress failed to pass the Troubled Asset Relief Program, and the stock market and other financial markets cratered.

There has been no discernible reaction in financial markets to a potential standoff over the debt limit so far. Credit default swaps on Treasury securities—the cost of insuring against a default by the Treasury—are currently close to a very low 5 basis points for one-year Treasuries, and less than 30 basis points for five-year securities. For context, in the summer of 2011 when brinkmanship around raising the debt limit was at its apex, CDS spreads on one-year Treasuries rose to as high as 80 basis points and those on five-year Treasuries to 65 basis points.

Markets are calm likely because it has become typical for Congress to run down the clock but in the end to raise the debt ceiling when absolutely necessary. It is thus widely expected that Congress will do so again. This is especially true now given that Republicans control both the executive and legislative branches of government. Investors cannot imagine that the deadline will be as disruptive as some recent experiences.

However, the House Republicans' inability to coalesce around a healthcare bill last week shows that policymaking is still rocky under a unified government. The longer it takes for policymakers to raise the debt limit, the more likely it will cost taxpayers money and harm the economy. And if policymakers fail to raise the limit before the Treasury runs out of cash and causes it to default on its obligations, it will be extraordinarily costly to taxpayers and do serious, even potentially catastrophic, damage to the economy.

Economic impact

The impact of political brinkmanship over the Treasury debt limit will show up first in higher interest rates. Just how costly this can be is evident from the reaction of Treasury investors during the last round of such brinkmanship in late 2013. A Moody's Analytics analysis of the period shows that investors nervous about a U.S. government default pushed 10-year Treasury yields up by 6 to 12 basis points at the height of their angst. Short-term interest rates also increased.[2]

Even though the Treasury ultimately did not default, and interest rates quickly fell back, the episode cost taxpayers an estimated nearly half-billion dollars in added interest costs. And this does not include the costs to households and businesses that also had to pay higher interest rates on the money they needed to borrow. Though these costs were relatively modest, they were unnecessarily incurred, and they surely would have been many multiple times greater if the Treasury actually had defaulted on its debt.

Brinkmanship around the debt limit will also quickly affect consumer and business sentiment and harm economic growth. Businesses will become more reluctant to invest and hire and entrepreneurs less likely to start companies. Financial institutions will be more circumspect about extending credit and households more cautious about their spending.

Uncertainty created by Washington is already very high, according to the Moody's Analytics political uncertainty index. The index is based on the CDS-implied probability of default on five-year Treasury bonds, the present value of future expiring tax provisions, and the share of businesses that cite legal and regulatory issues as their biggest problem in the Moody's Analytics weekly business survey. The index is set to equal zero in 2004-2005, near the end of the last business cycle. The higher the index, the greater the uncertainty.

The Moody's Analytics index rose significantly during the heated debate over the American Recovery and Reinvestment Act—the $830 billion fiscal stimulus—in early 2009. It surged during the budget debate in early 2010, and the Treasury debt-ceiling showdown in the summer of 2011 (see Chart 2). It hit a record high during the late 2013 government shutdown and has remained elevated ever since.

Political uncertainty is a corrosive on business investment, reduces hiring, and slows GDP growth. A statistical analysis shows that increased political uncertainty since the 2008 recession has lowered real GDP by close to $180 billion, reduced employment by 1.2 million jobs, and increased unemployment by 0.7 percentage point.[3] If not for the logjams in Washington in recent years, and if policy uncertainty had simply remained unchanged from its prerecession level, the economy would have returned to full employment nearly a year ago.[4]

Chart 2: Fiscal Uncertainty Remains Elevated

Fiscal policy uncertainty, 2004-2005=0

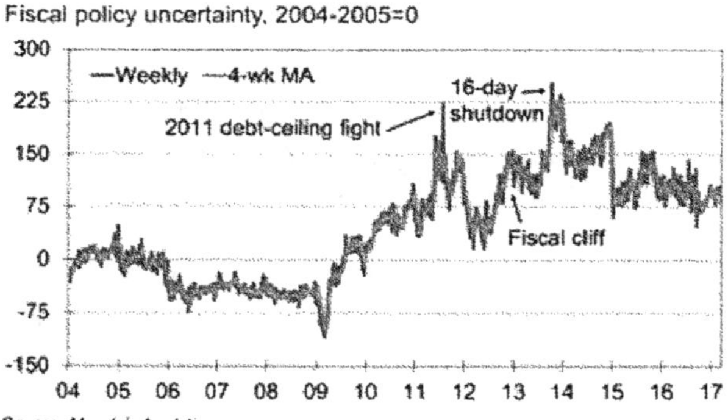

Source: Moody's Analytics

If the debt limit is not increased in time and the Treasury actually were to default, not only would interest rates and policy uncertainty soar, but the federal government would have to significantly cut back on its spending. Based on the timing of outlays and tax receipts, this would probably mean delaying by more than a week about $60 billion in payments due November 1 to Social Security recipients, veterans, and active-duty military. This would almost surely undermine consumer and business confidence.

If the impasse over the debt limit lasts through November, the Treasury will have no choice but to eliminate a cash deficit of approximately $130 billion by slashing government spending.

In contrast with previous recessions, the Federal Reserve and fiscal policymakers would have few tools available to cushion the blow. With Congress and the administration still at loggerheads, there would be no fiscal policy response, and with already very low short-term interest rates and a bloated Federal Reserve balance sheet, it is unclear how much the central bank could do to support the economy.

This would be a cataclysmic economic scenario. Based on simulations of the Moody's Analytics model of the U.S. economy, the downturn would be at least as severe as the Great Recession. That means real GDP would decline by as much as 5%, close to 10 million jobs would be lost, and unemployment would rise back close to double digits. With this economic backdrop, stock prices would likely be cut in half, wiping out about $10 trillion in household wealth. Treasury yields would likely spike, at least until the debt limit is increased and debt payments are resumed.

The path forward

Policymakers have yet to consider how they should go about increasing the debt limit. There are several approaches Republican leaders might take to address the issue, including raising the debt limit as part of a necessary spending bill, such as the spending legislation that will need to be enacted by September 30, the end of the current fiscal year. The debt limit could also be raised as part of the reconciliation process, and combining tax reform with a debt limit increase, for example. To do so, instructions to increase the debt limit would need to be included in the fiscal 2018 budget resolution sometime this summer.

Finally, Republican leaders could pass a debt limit increase as a standalone piece of legislation without any direct link to the budget process. Several recent debt limit increases have been passed this way. This option could be attractive if other legislation, such as tax reform, is not ready by the time the debt limit needs to be raised.

Budget reforms

Congress could also use this opportunity to eliminate the statutory debt ceiling. It is an idiosyncratic, anachronistic and, as has been demonstrated, potentially destructive rule that is detrimental to sound economic policy.

Short of a repeal of the debt ceiling, policymakers should consider strengthening the link between borrowing and tax and spending policy, by requiring "ability to pay" language in any legislation that adds to future deficits. Ability to pay is defined as sufficient projected tax revenue and borrowing authority to cover the current Congressional Budget Office deficit forecast. This requirement would be applied to all direct spending, taxation and annual appropriations bills. Any discrepancies that result from changes in the CBO forecast could be reconciled in the annual budget process.

The debt ceiling would still force lawmakers to think about the long-term fiscal impact of any legislation, but it would do so in the context of the spending and taxation bills that create the need for that debt. This proposal makes use of current CBO budget projections and scoring practices, and thus should cause no new compliance costs.

Another alternative would be to cap the ratio of the structural deficit to potential GDP for the coming year; as long as this remains below an agreed-upon threshold, the debt limit increase would be automatic.

Policymakers should also require the CBO and General Accounting Office to adopt fiscal-gap and generational accounting.[5] This provides a more accurate calculation of the nation's long-term fiscal obligations and thus would create the basis for sounder budgeting and fiscal decision-making.

The fiscal gap describes the difference between the present value of projected government expenditures, including interest and principal payments on outstanding federal debt, and taxes and other receipts, including income accruing from the government's ownership of financial assets. Generational accounting measures the burden of closing the fiscal gap on today's and tomorrow's children, assuming they must do so on their own and that the burden on each generation is proportional to its labor earnings.

Fiscal-gap accounting and generational accounting are comprehensive and forward-looking, and determine the sustainability of fiscal policy and the burden of that policy on future generations. Fiscal-gap accounting has already been adopted by the Social Security Trustees and Medicare Trustees and is becoming more widely used in other countries.

Taking these steps would restore the fundamental economic relationship between budgeting and borrowing, and reduce the risk that political brinkmanship could damage the full faith and credit of the U.S. or the stability of world financial markets.

Pro-growth policies

It is also important for lawmakers to address the nation's long-term fiscal challenges. Although the fiscal situation should be more or less stable during the next several years, the long-term outlook remains disconcerting. If Congress does not make significant changes to the tax code and entitlement programs, rising healthcare costs and an aging population will swamp the budget in coming decades.

Of course, the best way to address these looming challenges is to implement policies that will boost the economy's long-term growth rate. For every one-tenth of 1% increase in long-run GDP growth, the federal budget deficit over the next decade would be reduced by almost $300 billion. Thus policies that increase GDP growth from say 2% per annum—the current consensus outlook for real GDP growth over the next decade—to 2.5% per annum, for example, would reduce annual budget deficits by a sizable $150 billion.

To achieve such a boost in the economy's long-run growth and improvement in the nation's finances, three key policies should be implemented: revenue-neutral corporate tax reform, immigration reform that significantly increases the number of legal immigrants permitted into the country, and a significant expansion in infrastructure spending.

Corporate tax reform

Revenue-neutral corporate tax reform that lowers marginal corporate tax rates and is paid for by scaling back or eliminating tax preferences in the code or other sources of revenue would support growth by improving the competitiveness of U.S. businesses. As part of corporate tax reform, policymakers should replace our current worldwide taxation system with a territorial system that has a minimum tax on overseas earnings. Multinationals should also be encouraged to repatriate their now sizable pile of overseas profits with a lower tax rate.

However, paying for any cuts to marginal rates will be difficult. Every 1-percentage point reduction in the corporate tax rate costs the Treasury approximately $120 billion over a 10-year period on a static basis. Thus, reducing the top rate from its current 35% to 25%, for example, would cost $1.2 trillion. The lower marginal rates will result in a stronger economy, and thus on a dynamic basis the cost will be closer to an estimated $900 billion, but this is still a very big number and a heavy lift for policymakers.

A phased-in so-called border adjustment tax would be a reasonable way to raise the needed revenue. Simply put, the idea behind the tax is to require all imported goods and services to effectively pay the corporate tax, but exempt all exports from the tax. Because the U.S. runs a close to $500 billion annual trade deficit, the tax would raise the revenue needed to lower the marginal rate to 25%.

The principal downside to the border adjustment tax is the uncertain incidence of the tax. That is, it is unclear who ultimately will pay for it. Much of the tax will be borne by foreign companies selling their wares in the U.S., but it could also be partially borne by U.S. consumers via higher costs for imported goods. U.S. retailers may also feel some ill effects. In theory, if phased in, U.S. consumers and retailers should not be harmed, but this depends on a range of assumptions including the impact of the tax on the value of the U.S. dollar. So in practice, we cannot know for sure what the incidence will be.

Immigration reform

Reform of the nation's immigration laws would provide an even more effective way of boosting long-term economic growth. The Border Security, Economic Opportunity, and Immigration Modernization Act of 2013 is a good example of such reform. This legislation—also known as the Gang of Eight bill for the eight senators, including Republicans and Democrats, who crafted the legislation—passed the Senate in a bipartisan vote but stalled in the House and never became law.

This legislation expands existing employment-based immigration, including exempting from the cap on green cards foreigners with STEM graduate degrees or doctorates in any field. The number of temporary immigration visas for skilled and unskilled workers also increases. It would create a points-based immigration track that would reward individuals with greater education, English fluency, and other factors. Family-based immigration would be expanded by uncapping the annual number of green cards that can be issued to spouses and unmarried children of existing legal permanent residents. And perhaps most controversially, the reform includes a path to legalization for undocumented immigrants living in the country who meet certain criteria.

The Congressional Budget Office's economic analysis of this legislation found that it would increase legal immigration to the U.S. by approximately 1 million per year. Within a decade, the U.S. population would be about 3% larger than it would be without the change in immigration law. The legislation would result in a substantial increase in the number of both high-skilled and low-skilled immigrant workers.

According to the CBO, this legislation would increase real GDP by a substantial 3.3% within a decade compared with what GDP would have been without the change. The increase in population also lifts the labor force and employment. There would be close to 6 million more jobs in 10 years, as the additional population would add to the demand for goods and services and, in turn, the demand for labor. Productivity would also receive a measurable boost, as the "immigration of highly skilled immigrants would tend to generate additional technological advancements, such as new inventions and improvements in production processes."[6]

Infrastructure investment

A significant increase in public infrastructure investment would also support stronger longer-term growth. The federal government spends approximately $100 billion per year on infrastructure, mostly on transportation and water systems.[7] Federal financial support for infrastructure should be substantially increased via more direct spending and the formation of an infrastructure bank.

The bank would provide direct loans, loan guarantees, and other forms of credit enhancement, which would support hundreds of billions in more infrastructure spending. If fashioned off the Transportation Infrastructure Finance and Innovation Act program, the bank could fund a significant amount of additional investment. For example, if the bank received $25 billion in seed capital, it could support as much as $250 billion in federal loans over a five-year period. Those loans, in turn, could make up approximately one-third of total project costs, so in all the infrastructure bank could support as much as $750 billion in total additional infrastructure development. Although to be sure, the operation and success of such an infrastructure bank involves significant uncertainties.

An infrastructure bank could also help administer a Build America Bonds program, which was successful in financing a substantial amount of infrastructure development in the wake of the financial crisis.[8] This would be a significant change in the tax preferences that the federal government offers to buyers of municipal bonds, which are often issued to finance highway construction projects. Tax-exempt bonds are a relatively inefficient way to subsidize state and local governments' investment in infrastructure, because the revenue cost to the federal government may substantially exceed the interest-cost subsidy provided to the state and local governments.

Possible budget changes

Even if policymakers are able to implement these pro-growth policies, to fully address the nation's long-term fiscal problems, policymakers will still need to implement cuts in government spending and increases in tax revenues. What follows are a few suggestions.

Unfortunately, as economist like to say, there is no free lunch; any change in tax and spending policy requires hard choices. These suggestions significantly reduce future budget deficits, have limited broader economic consequences, and are sensitive to the distributional impacts on different groups. Taken together, these suggested changes will reduce budget deficits over the next decade by close to $1 trillion. But even more will need to be done, particularly with regard to the growth in future healthcare costs, but that is a subject for another day.

Increase the maximum taxable earnings for the Social Security payroll tax.

When payroll taxes for Social Security were first collected in 1937, about 92% of earnings from jobs covered by the program were below the maximum taxable amount. This has slipped substantially over the past more than a decade. Even as the maximum increases with the growth in average earnings, earnings for the highest-paid workers have grown much faster because of the skewing in incomes. In 2016, only 82% of earnings from employment covered by Social Security fell below the maximum taxable amount.

The suggestion would be to increase the taxable share of earnings from jobs covered by Social Security to 90%. The maximum taxable amount would increase to $245,000 in calendar year 2017. In later years, the maximum would grow at the same rate as average wages, as it does under current law.

Implementing such a policy change would increase federal revenues by an estimated $648 billion over the next decade, according to the Joint Committee on Taxation.[9]

Use the chained consumer price index measure of inflation to index Social Security and other mandatory programs, and some parameters in the tax code.

Cost-of-living adjustments for Social Security and other federal programs are indexed to increases in traditional measures of the consumer price index. The CPI measures overall inflation and is calculated by the Bureau of Labor Statistics. In addition to the traditional measures of the CPI, that agency computes another measure of inflation—the chained CPI—designed to account for changes in spending patterns and to eliminate several types of statistical biases that exist in the traditional CPI measures.

The suggestion would replace the traditional CPI beginning in 2018 with the chained CPI for indexing cost-of-living adjustments for Social Security and parameters of other programs. This change would also apply to various parameters in the tax code, such as income thresholds that divide the tax brackets. The chained CPI has grown by an average of about 0.25 percentage point more slowly per year over the past decade than the traditional CPI measures have, and the gap is likely to persist. Therefore, the option would reduce federal spending and increase revenues, and the benefits to the budget would grow each year as the effects of the change compounded.

Implementing such a policy change would lower federal spending by $182 billion through 2026, according to the CBO. And according to the Joint Committee on Taxation, it would increase federal revenues by $157 billion over the same period.

Convert the mortgage interest deduction into a 15% tax credit.

Homeowners can deduct the mortgage interest they pay on up to $1.1 million in mortgage debt if they itemize their deductions. Like all itemized deductions, the value is reduced as the homeowners' adjusted gross income increases above specified thresholds. Homeowners benefit from this deduction through higher house prices, as the value of the deduction is largely capitalized in house prices. And generally wealthier homeowners benefit, as they are the ones likely to itemize on their tax returns.

The suggestion is to gradually convert the tax deduction for mortgage interest to a 15% nonrefundable tax credit. This change would be phased in over six years, beginning in 2017. By 2022, the deduction would be replaced by a 15% credit; the maximum amount of mortgage debt that could be included in the credit calculation would be $500,000; and the credit could be applied only to interest on debt incurred on a first home. This change would promote homeownership, as lower- and middle-income households who are more likely to benefit are also more likely to be renters.

This suggestion would raise $105 billion in revenues over the next decade, according to the Joint Committee on Taxation. The increase in revenue would be substantially greater in subsequent decades.

Conclusions

Washington's budget battles in recent years have been painful to watch and harmful to the economy. Political brinkmanship creates significant uncertainty and much anxiety among consumers, businesses and investors, impairing their willingness to spend, hire and invest.

Despite these political headwinds, the economic expansion is nearly 8 years old, making it the second longest in the nation's economic history. The economy is at full employment for the first time in a decade, and the benefits of the stronger economy are finally beginning to accrue to lower- and middle-income households. Business balance sheets are about as strong as they have ever been, the banking system is well capitalized, and households have significantly reduced their debt loads.

This is an opportune time for policymakers to address the nation's long-standing fiscal challenges. This includes eliminating the statutory debt limit; adopting fiscal gap and generational accounting; implementing pro-growth policies such as revenue-neutral corporate tax reform, immigration reform, and infrastructure investment; and making some modest adjustments to tax and spending policies.

Accomplishing this will require some deft policymaking, but it would put the American economy and the nation's finances on a solid foundation for decades to come.

---

[1] These are similar to estimates done by the Congressional Budget Office.

[2] The referenced Moody's Analytics study is available upon request.

[3] These results are based on a structural vector autoregressive model of the U.S. economy. The model is used to estimate the extent to which surprise changes in political uncertainty produce changes in GDP, unemployment, the hiring rate, investment, jobs, and several other economic variables.

[4] It is difficult to statistically distinguish between political uncertainty and policy uncertainty. Political uncertainty is created by political brinkmanship and dysfunction in government. Policy uncertainty is created by potential changes in government spending, taxes and regulation. The 2011 showdown over the Treasury debt limit was especially hard on the economy, as it created a great deal of political uncertainty but also involved large changes to spending and tax policy. The current government funding and debt limit debates may have less economic impact, as they appear to involve more political than policy uncertainty. Despite current legislative efforts to defund the Affordable Care Act, such defunding seems very unlikely, and no other major policy changes are being debated, at least so far. Also mitigating the economic impact of the current debate is that businesspeople, consumers and investors appear to be increasingly desensitized to the political vitriol with each budget battle.

[5] This proposal is part of the INFORM Act.

[6] CBO continues that "total factor productivity (TFP, the average real output per unit of combined labor and capital services) would be higher by roughly 0.7% in 2023 than what would occur under current law. The increase in TFP would make workers and capital alike more productive, leading to higher GDP, higher wages, and higher interest rates."

[7] According to a CBO analysis, an additional approximately $300 billion per year is spent on infrastructure by state and local governments.

[8] Build America Bonds, which supported more than $180 billion in infrastructure spending during the financial crisis, are a more efficient way of helping to finance infrastructure spending than traditional tax-exempt municipal debt, as tax-exempt municipal debt ends up benefiting not just infrastructure projects but also high-income purchasers of the debt. See the statement of Frank Sammartino, assistant director for Tax Analysis of the Congressional Budget Office, in a hearing of the Senate Finance Committee.

[9] These estimates account for the reduction in individual income tax revenues that would result from employers' shifting some labor compensation from a taxable to a nontaxable form.

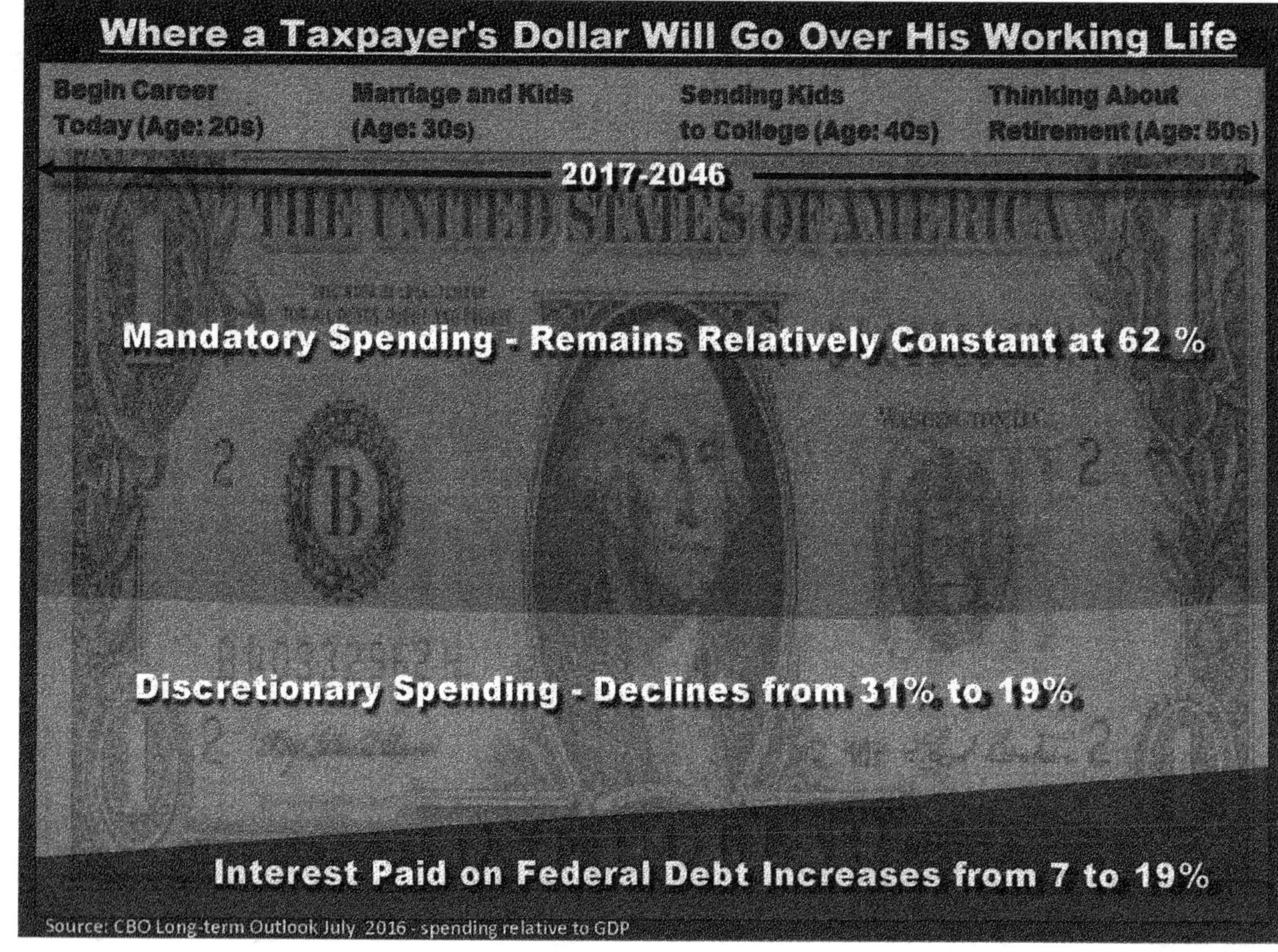

Where a Taxpayer's Dollar Will Go Over His Working Life
Begin Career Today (Age: 20s)
Marriage and Kids (Age: 30s)
Sending Kids to College (Age: 40s)
Thinking About Retirement (Age: 50s)
2017-2046
Mandatory Spending - Remains Relatively Constant at 62 %
Discretionary Spending - Declines from 31% to 19%
Interest Paid on Federal Debt Increases from 7 to 19%
Source: CBO Long-term Outlook July 2016 - spending relative to GDP